# ON GUARD FOR THEE
## CANADIAN PEACEKEEPING MISSIONS

## by

## Matthew Bin

**BookLand press**

**Toronto, Canada**
**2007**

**Published by:**
**BookLand Press Inc.**
**6021 Yonge Street**
**Suite 1010**
**Toronto, Ontario M2M 3W2**
**Canada**
**www.booklandpress.com**


Editor:  Robert Morgan

Printed and bound in Canada.


**Library and Archives Canada Cataloguing in Publication**

Bin, Matthew, 1973-
      On guard for thee : Canadian peacekeeping missions / by
Matthew Bin.

ISBN 978-0-9783793-2-2


      1. Peacekeeping forces, Canadian - Biography.  2.
Peacekeeping forces - Canada - History.  I. Title.

JZ6377.C3B55 2007          355.3'57          C2007-905615-6

**IN HONOUR
OF THOSE WHO SERVED**

**IN MEMORY
OF THOSE WHO FELL**

Should the Security Council consider that measures provided for in Article 41 would be inadequate or have proved to be inadequate, it may take such action by air, sea, or land forces as may be necessary to maintain or restore international peace and security. Such action may include demonstrations, blockade, and other operations by air, sea, or land forces of Members of the United Nations.

~ *Article 42, Chapter 6*
*Charter of the United Nations*

# INTRODUCTION

The peace operations that Canada has undertaken since World War II have been a source of pride, honour, and national identity for our nation. Over 120,000 Canadian Armed Forces personnel have served overseas in peace operations under the UN and NATO. Nearly 120 Canadians have sacrificed their lives on United Nations peacekeeping missions, in addition to over 60 men and women in the ongoing conflict in Afghanistan.

This book brings together the voices of soldiers from major Canadian international commitments from the deployment for the Gulf War in 1990 to the operations in Afghanistan and elsewhere that continue today. The stories are those of regular soldiers from every region of Canada. Some were young privates or corporals at the beginning of their careers; others were senior officers nearing retirement. All served overseas amid conflict and strife, and all wore the maple leaf on their shoulder.

This is not a history of Canadian peacekeeping, or a complete picture of Canadian military operations in the modern age. Instead, this book portrays, on an honest and individual level, the reality of peacekeeping as the soldiers saw it. Together, they tell the story of the Canadian peacekeeper's experience in the modern age.

This book covers a period of great change, both in Canada's military and international position and in UN peacekeeping in general. As the Cold War ended, the need to commit our military to NATO in Europe was drastically reduced, and eventually disappeared; the size and strength of our military diminished accordingly.

Meanwhile, new conflicts were arising throughout the world. About half of all UN peacekeeping operations in history have their start dates between 1988 and 1998, and Canada was committed in some capacity to nearly all of them. Canada made significant contributions in the former Yugoslavia and in Africa, as well as missions in Asia and, closer to home, in Haiti. Canadians have repeatedly received accolades for their service on their missions.

I interviewed veterans through the spring and summer of

2007, some in person and others on the phone. I asked them to simply tell me about their experiences, good and bad, from the preparation for their mission to their return home and beyond. Once the ball was rolling, it was often hard to stop them—if there's one thing I know about the military, it's that soldiers tell stories.

What I did not anticipate was the deep, wholehearted commitment, in every veteran I interviewed, to helping the less fortunate around the world. This was not some abstract notion of compassion or charity: they saw the worst the world had to offer, and they did everything in their power—to the point of risking their own lives—to change it.

In every country where they are deployed, in extremely harsh conditions, amid squalor and danger, Canadians put the people around them, ordinary citizens in a foreign country, first. They bring food and medical help to those who need it, they protect those in peril, and they often spend their scant free time helping to bring something to people who have so little—a roof over their heads, food and water, even toys for small children.

This deep emotional connection with the people they serve often leads to difficulties once the work has ended. Many of the soldiers I interviewed mentioned that they did not want to leave the areas where they were deployed, because they felt they could continue to do good if they stayed. There was a lot of pride, too, in programs that continued after they left, programs they created to better the lives of the people they saw all around them.

The darker side of these emotional bonds, though, are the psychological scars that some of them will bear forever. Many peacekeepers came back irreversibly changed, some so severely that they required time and help merely to readjust to their lives back in Canada. As more than one peacekeeper said, the Canadian Forces is taking much better care of its soldiers now—but we'd better prepare for those who are coming back from Afghanistan, as they're going to have their share of problems, too.

That, in fact, is the purpose this book was written. Our pride as a country in our peacekeepers' service too easily leads us to sentimentalize their work. It's easy to imagine the square-jawed Canadian soldier, in a blue helmet, standing on guard for us. It's a little more difficult to imagine the garbage and sewage, the angry mobs, the landmines and machine guns and tripwires, the people hacked and shot and murdered before their eyes. It's hard to know what they go through without asking them.

So here are the words of the peacekeepers themselves.

# 1

# RAMP-UP

Most of a soldier's career—years upon years for many—is spent training. Once the mission is set, though, the training moves to a new level. The modern period introduced new challenges for the armed forces, as more and more reservists were introduced into international missions, and missions required new training to face situations and threats never encountered before.

## Cambodia, 1994

They said they were starting up a tour in Cambodia and they needed transport guys who are master corporals to go over to be section commanders. They were woefully short on section commanders who'd been on other tours. I wasn't in that role any more, but my initial trade had been MSC (Mission Support Centre) Ops, so I knew the logistics branch and the way things worked. I was a master corporal, and I'd been on a tour prior, so I fit the bill. Because I didn't want to get railroaded again, I said, "Okay, if I sign up for this, I want be sure that I'm going." And they said, "No, you're definitely going. There's no ifs, ands, or buts about it. You're going."

The next day, I was back on a bus back to Calgary, where the pre-training for Cambodia was. One of the interesting things about the training at that time was, it was the middle of winter, and to train for Yugoslavia in the winter and early spring, they sent the guys from Winnipeg to Coronado, California. We're going to the jungle, and where do we go for our pre-workout training? Suffield in January. Typical army mentality—drive with the lights on during the day and turn them off at night.

## Former Yugoslavia, 1992

I remember when I was told we were going into Yugoslavia, my immediate thought was great, we're going to finally get to use all this training that we've had. My specialty was bomb disposal and mine awareness; in fact, I was one of the highest qualified in all of the Canadian Forces at that time.

When a friend of mine in 4th Combat Engineer Regiment

told me they were being moved in their entirety to Yugoslavia, he immediately thought of me. It was quite funny—he sent a message up to where I was stationed, requesting a combat engineer with the following qualifications, and he had copied everything that I had. Of course, there was only the one in the entire Canadian Forces that met those requirements, so when I was called into the Commanding Officer's office and read this message, I said, "Sir, I volunteer," and of course away I went. I was very happy, too, to have others from my troop go with me as well. It was a bit of extra comradeship, and I knew who they were and knew their capabilities.

I must say the training that we had was exceptional. We all had chances to go to the States and take special training with them, and also to England to take special training with them. It wasn't particularly for the Yugoslavia mission, it was training for war, and also for peacetime operations. When we went into Yugoslavia it came in very handy.

The training we had here in Canada was outstanding, we couldn't have asked for better. The only thing that we weren't prepared for was the actual type of munitions. But really, the entire world works off a very similar method of arming and disarming and actuating mines, so it's very similar almost everywhere. Some kind of pressure has to be put on a mine to set it off, some kind of a wire has to be pulled in order to activate a fuse, so it was all pretty much the same. Nowadays, they've got all kinds of extra things, you can fire them remotely and so on.

# Afghanistan, 2006-07

We trained with guys who had been in Afghanistan before and they didn't mess around. Bring it to the next level. In the reserves it's not the same, they're very polite, but they're not that aggressive. They're not thinking, "I'm about to die." They don't understand that. "I'm about to die."

Training in (CFB) Wainwright, we were moving as a troop all the time, a lot more than we would end up moving in Afghanistan. They'd set up all these scenarios where guys would attack us. They'd kill our leadership, our officers and so on, and see how everybody else reacted. Or they'd send people to approach our position. When do you stop them? When do you shoot at them? Then it started to slow down for us. We'd just sit in a FOB (Forward Operating Base), sit in our positions and fire the howitzers.

But there was good training there, good training on the guns. A lot of experience on the mortars. A lot of us had never used mortars before; I had never used mortars before. It's pretty easy to learn for artillerymen and we used them a lot in Afghanistan.

In the reserves, I've never set up as fast as we set up in training for Afghanistan. And really when you came to Afghanistan, we trained to a level in Canada that was unrealistic in a way; we just don't move around that much.

## Cambodia, 1993-94

We only had about two months—we started in September, and we were gone by the end of October. But that was the early days, post-Germany, so they assumed that you were already trained and ready to go. And because it wasn't such a hot spot—it wasn't Bosnia, it wasn't Somalia—we had minimal weapons training, mostly driving training. We were a transport battalion, we were called 92 Transport Company of Op Marquis.

We did our eight weeks' training, then our six weeks' vacation leave, and one week pre-train, and we were off. You could actually research the date, because we left Trenton the day after Toronto won the World Series the first time. I was actually a huge Dave Justice fan at the time, and I ended up almost hanging out of a window because I had a hundred and fifty bucks riding on that game.

## Golan Heights, 1999

The prep for the mission was very little to be perfectly honest. In Canada we have a lot of experience with putting the battle groups together and training them as battle groups going into Bosnia and stuff like that. But the Golan Heights had been ongoing since '73. It's staffed by individual augmentations. They pull a clerk here, pull a clerk here, across the whole country, they attend a two week basic peacekeeping course in Kingston, which pretty much just gives them a background of what UN peacekeeping is all about. Then they're flown over individually, they arrive in Tel Aviv, and they're brought to the base. There's a couple days more of training on the base, but that's more sort of base-specific to where they are in the Golan Heights.

I was going in as the operations officer, so I was responsible for the training these people received when they got there. So having gone through the training in Kingston and what we received there, I was able to see where the gaps were and incorporated that in exercises through our six months there, as well as incorporated better training when the next group came in, because they rotated every three months. Half of the contingent rotated every three months, so that a full rotation happened every six months. You had a number of people with experience that way, and it stayed through the next rotation of people.

## Afghanistan, 2003

It was pretty quick for the Third Battalion to go into Kandahar into Operation Apollo, which was 2002. Then it was 2003, summer 2003, by the time Roto 0 arrived in Kabul. So I guess between September 2001 and July 2003 there wasn't an awful lot of time.

For myself, it wasn't a significant amount of training. My battalion group had gone through the whole combat operations training as part of a brigade training in 2003, so they were fairly well-equipped to deal with combat operations in Kabul.

Because I was in the national command element, the training I got mostly goes back to command staff college in Kingston, because that was my function, in an operational setting. I had already served a couple of years in a brigade headquarters staff so I knew operational focus at brigade and higher levels.

Roto 0 never gets the same amount of training because it's hard to predict what a Roto 0 will need. The mission hadn't started up yet. We're obviously not getting feedback from the

French or Germans in theatre about what kind of training is really required for framework patrolling and security assistance in Kabul. We went up to Petawawa, we did less than 30 days' training, went on pre-deployment leave, and we deployed into theatre.

# DEPLOYMENT

Leaving home to go on a mission—regardless of how peaceful or dangerous it's expected to be—is full of emotion. A soldier knows what he or she is leaving behind, but is also excited about the mission that is about to start. And the trip from Canada to the eventual destination overseas is sometimes an adventure in itself. One thing seems certain—it's almost impossible to prepare for the first time your boots hit the ground in a foreign country.

# Cyprus, 1991

Nothing prepares you for your first tour, coming out of high school and hitting the ground in a foreign country. You don't speak the language, you don't know what to expect. You get off the plane, instantly you're getting your equipment issued, you've got to get your blue helmet instead of your green one, you're getting your Kevlar vest, you're getting your weapons, signing off for your kit, so it's pretty fast and dramatic.

The first 24 hours was pretty dramatic for me because inside of six hours from landing on the island I was thrown in the observation post for the next shift change, and I was there for a twelve-hour shift. That was my first 18 hours.

# Cambodia, 1994

Getting to Cambodia, we hadn't moved any troops from any Canadian staging area since Korea. Rather than paying the money to fly that many troops commercially, they were going to look at their military capability. Pretty much all that was at their disposal was the old 707s, which had been taken out of service because they were so old and unsafe to fly.

At that time the military didn't have any commercial style aircraft to fly people. Prior to that, they had those 707s and they were in an airline configuration and they flew back and forth across Canada every day, moving troops from place to place to place, going over to Germany and that kind of thing. When the 707s exceeded their maximum lifespan and serviceability, they took them out of commission. So now, any time troops had to move across Canada it was all commercial or on a Herc or whatever. Well, they pulled one of these 707s out of retirement.

The unit had all congregated in Calgary for pre-training. And when they brought out this plane out of mothballs, they decided they were not allowed to fly it for longer than eight hours in a stretch without an inspection of the aircraft.

Essentially, what that meant was instead of going to Hong Kong and then to Phnom Penh, which would be the most logical route for a transport craft to go, we went from Calgary to Honolulu. We stayed overnight in Honolulu and they put up about 130 to 150 of us in a hotel. Imagine how much it cost them to get that many rooms! Then the plane had to have an inspection, so it couldn't go beyond that.

The next day, the inspection done, we hopped on the plane and flew to Anderson Air Force base in Guam and holed up there for a day while another inspection was done on the aircraft. Then from Guam, we flew to Thailand. We spent another day there, but by this time, they'd come up with a Hercules aircraft with UN colours, and that flew us the last bit into Phnom Penh.

## Rwanda, 1994-95

I went to Rwanda from Somalia. I had been on a week-long trip visiting prisons and police stations. I was just coming back on a Friday afternoon, and when my helicopter landed there was a Canadian officer there waiting for me. He said, "You heard about Rwanda?" I said yes, I heard it during my trip. I had been talking to my wife on the telephone on that trip and she had told me everything has broken loose in Rwanda. And he said, "You'd better start packing your things because you're going there. You're leaving Monday or Tuesday." Another 48 hours later, I was on my way to Rwanda.

When I left Mogadishu to go to Rwanda, although I was aware in general of the situation, that the president had been killed, his plane shot down, and then they had started some massacres, I never thought or imagined the degree of or the gravity of the situation until I arrived in Kigali.

# Qatar, 1990

It was quite a strange deployment. We were in Baden (Germany), which was about 75 kilometres north of Lahr. We travelled down there all the time and did all the pre-training. But in the actual deployment, they came up and picked us up by bus and took us just north of there to a United States air base, and we flew from there into Zurich, in Switzerland. We flew out of Switzerland in the Hercs.

The recce (reconnaissance) team that went over, there were 14 of us initially, we flew over in one Herc. We landed in Cyprus and did a run-up on the airplane and refuelled and so on. We were there for about two hours. Then we took off from Cyprus and we flew down over Egypt because we didn't want to get involved with any Iraqi aircraft at that time. We were unescorted at that time; we didn't have any CF-18 escorts. So we flew basically over neutral territory. Of course, all of this had to be pre-planned and worked out in advance, so Egypt knew we were flying over. And I got to see the pyramids from the sky, which was very nice. The sun was just going down.

# Afghanistan (from Canada), 2005

At Christmas, I bought him a new wedding band and I proposed to him again—to give him a new wedding band, and keep his old wedding band for just in case, because I wanted to give that wedding band to the boys. Our son had severe health problems, and I wondered then if our son would be here a year from now, if my husband would be here a year from now, if we'd be celebrating in '06.

We left on a Sunday and he left on the Monday. He called me at six o'clock in the morning the day of our son's medical tests, which was the Thursday morning. And Thursday morning was Thursday night to them. It comes through an Ottawa line, area code 613, and I was freaked out because I thought they were trying to call me to say he was dead. I'd been with our son and I didn't have the cell phone right by me, so I didn't get his call until the fifth time and he was just saying that he was in the country; he was out there somewhere, he couldn't tell me where.

## Cambodia, 1994

That night, we'd been flying all that time, we were tired, we were shown to our bunks, and got set up and basically everyone went to ground right away. I don't think we were in bed more than 45 minutes and all kinds of gunfire erupted outside. For many people it was the first time they'd heard gunfire other than on a range. I could just imagine if there'd been a camera on the wall of the barracks, it must've looked like the keystone cops.

We were in what amounts to a combat zone, but at that time, they still had the exercise mentality when it came to weapons control. We didn't have our weapons by our side. They were locked in weapons racks each night, and the ammunition was in a different area. If you needed your weapon, one guy had the key and had to come and unlock the weapons, distribute them and get the ammunition, just like you would in (CFB) Wainwright—only right now, there are bullets flying and we haven't got our weapons.

We got the weapons unlocked and we were running outside. We had our flak jackets on and everything. As we're running outside, we're hearing people yelling, "Check fire! Check fire!" What it turned out to be was a Tet celebration. It was Tet and nobody had told us, and they celebrate by shooting into the air. There are probably three or four houses within 50 metres of the fence line of the camp. A colonel in the CPAF (Cambodian People's Armed Forces) lived about 15 to 20 metres of the fence line and he was one of the ones shooting into the air.

I think that the only reason that none of the Cambodians got shot that night was because it was such a shock to our troops. We were a transport battalion. We weren't infantry. I think the hesitation within the non-combat arms was the only reason someone didn't get shot that night. Everybody had a good chuckle about it afterwards, but it was pretty serious at the time.

# Haiti, 1995-96

We went by Herc, it was a Canadian C-130 aircraft that left
Trenton. We got into Haiti, and the weather in Haiti was extremely
hot. It was over 45 degrees. At that point I said I would never be
able to survive in there. But believe it or not you get used to it.
You drink a lot of water and you get used to it. But over there, you
didn't have a choice of weather. It was 45 degrees, seven days a
week. And even in the winter the lowest that it went there was 35
degrees, 40 degrees maybe. Maybe 5 degrees difference.

# Rwanda, 1994-95

There were two other officers with me, and we were flown from
Mogadishu to Nairobi, Kenya, and from Nairobi directly into
Kigali. I remember it was raining, and we arrived there at about
two o'clock in the afternoon. There was kind of a light rain and
the airport was closed to all civilian traffic, so there were only a
few aircraft still flying in and out of the airport. The French army
was evacuating its expatriates, the UN contingent was reducing
their forces considerably, so the airport was full of soldiers and
expatriates and you name it.

When I got off the aircraft, I walked into the airport hoping
to find a toilet. Normally when you go into the terminal you find
a toilet. Absolutely not, everything was broken or already full or
whatever. Anyway, I had to go outside somewhere between two
vehicles and do whatever I had to do before I got into the vehicle
that was taking me to the UN headquarters in Kigali. So that was
my arrival. The lack of toilet facilities and there was no running
water, everything had been broken, that was the start.

There were some officers waiting for us and we were
transported to UN headquarters which was about two or three
kilometres from the airport. At that time we could hear gunfire
here and there, going off almost continuously. So we got into the
UN Headquarters and General Dallaire was there and welcomed
us, and of course he was extremely busy. He interviewed us in a
group, and I said I was a military police officer, but there was no

police force or UN police force, they were evacuated with many other soldiers already. So he said, "I'm gonna give you the job of a staff officer, this is what I want you to do until further notice," and he did the same thing with the other two.

When the three of us arrived, in Rwanda there were only two other Canadians: General Dallaire and another officer. So when we arrived, those two plus the three of us, we were five. The Belgian contingent was in the process of finishing evacuating its contingent, because of the ten Belgian soldiers that had been killed. What remained in Rwanda were the soldiers of the various countries that have provided the peacekeepers to the force, maybe 1500 peacekeepers from different countries, mainly from Ghana and from Tunisia, but from 15 countries. Some countries had only two or three people, but Ghana had about 500.

The five Canadians were all officers, all at the rank of Major except of course General Dallaire, and we were all working as staff officers in the UN headquarters. Each was given a specific job. There was no work for me at all as a military police officer. Before the beginning of hostilities there had been a small UN police force, but they had been evacuated somehow with some other UN soldiers for whatever reason. So when I arrived there in fact I was the only military police officer in Rwanda, so there was nobody for me to command. At that time we were not worried about policing UN forces, we were in the middle of a war.

Dallaire told me, you will be with the transport section, looking after the UN vehicles that have been abandoned all over the place in Kigali. He said you're going to try to recover most of them so if we need to evacuate by land or by road, you're going to have as many vehicles ready as possible.

I had to try to gather and survey all the vehicles that were available to us and in good running condition and try to gather them all in one spot so that I could tell the General yes we have 55 ten-ton trucks, we have so many four-wheel-drive, we have so many of this, so many of that, and they are in working condition.

When I arrived, I remember, let's say within the first hour of being inside the UN Headquarters, the UN building headquarters, I could smell something rotten, you know, a strange smell. So I asked one of the officers there, "What is that strange smell?"

He said, "Just over the wall there, you see that smoke? They are burning a pile of dead bodies." This was exactly what it was. That smell has remained with me up to today.

The job as transport officer lasted for only for a week or so. I had managed to gather quite a few vehicles and produce reports, so many of this and that, with the co-operation of other people. We had a briefing from General Dallaire to his key staff officers in the morning and at night, seven in the morning and seven at night, and one night Dallaire, who knew me from a long time ago, without even asking me, announced to everybody, as of that time, I was the UN spokesman for the mission. I said, "Oh, my God, I'm an old policeman." He said, "I know you can do it, I've talked to New York and talked to the head of the civilian office in Kigali, and he said you're up to the job."

Dallaire had a lot of telephone calls from ITV, the CBC, whatever, which he used to do himself because there was no UN spokesman for the mission. Before the war this was just a little mission, almost forgotten by everybody. Dallaire and the head of the civilian component of the UN mission were receiving dozens and dozens of requests for interviews now, and this was taking up a lot of valuable time for the general. So he said as of now, that's it, you're up, we're gonna set up a direct line to Canada and to the outside world in your little office, which was also my bedroom, and here are a few telephone numbers, start talking to them. Do the best you can. And I did that for the next few months.

# Qatar, 1990

Our Canadian task group landed in a place called Doha, in Qatar, around midnight. It was hot, sweltering, and humid. The chaps who were there already, there were a couple of chaps on the ground, they were on about their third uniform that day. We were literally drenched by the time we got off the aircraft.

We were pretty much isolated, about five miles out of Doha itself, in a very deserted area, if I can use that word in the desert. In fact, when we arrived, this camp was actually a dumping ground for refuse. There was even the corpse of an old horse. I personally have no sense of smell whatsoever but I gather that this thing was quite hummy.

The horse luckily still had the steel wire rope wrapped around its hoofs. That was the method they used to drag it into this area, and I managed to convince one of my master corporals to drive a front-end loader and I hooked the carcass to the hitch.

When he started to move it, forty thousand flies came out to see what was going on, and went immediately to the driver of the front-end loader. Flies can move faster than a front-end loader towing a horse, so he was pretty much surrounded by these millions and millions of flies. It wasn't very pleasant, you can imagine. We finally got it outside the grounds, and everyone was much happier with it on the outside.

## Bosnia, 2001

We flew direct from Trenton to Zagreb in a Canadian Forces Airbus. It was pretty straight. You could tell you weren't in Kansas any more when the plane is taxiing down the runway after landing and you see all the Russian helicopters and the Croatian markings. I'd never seen the Russian attack helicopters before, and I thought, whoa, I guess I'm not in Canada anymore. That was the eye opener. But it was pretty straightforward, because we were a NATO force and we weren't in combat so there was no secrecy.

It was what I expected, but it was a shock nonetheless. I mean, you train your whole life, and then you get on the ground and you see the carnage. Just driving by all the villages that don't exist any more was a real eye-opener. Real people lived here, and now there's nobody. That was the big welcome to Bosnia. Then the bus ride up and down the switchbacks and you're going oh my god, I hope the driver knows what he's doing. A beautiful country, it's just screwed up.

# Afghanistan, 2003

We went through Camp Mirage in the undisclosed Middle-Eastern country. We arrived in a 52 degree heat, got our personal weapons issued, our flak vests issued, and then essentially put our heads down for three hours until the Herc flight was going to leave.

Tactically flying into Kabul, doing weaves and turns, that's the first time I've actually done that in a Hercules aircraft. After landing in Kabul airport, we were rushed off the plane into the airport. They broke the ammunition open, and we loaded our magazines as fast as we could, signed for our ammunition, got into armoured vehicles, hunkered down and combat-drove through the streets of Kabul until we were through the doors in Camp Julien. Suddenly we were in theatre.

Quite a culture shock, to the point where people got into camp and they were all bewildered because all of a sudden, you're in a safe Canadian walled camp. People wanted to look over the walls to see what they'd come through and how they'd gotten there.

# Sri Lanka, 2005

Regardless of what the press says, we were on the ground very quickly and doing our humanitarian operations very quickly when we got on the ground there. They think it took us a long time. It took us a long time to get all of our equipment into the theatre, but as soon as we had our main people, our doctors and medical people, in the operation, they had their black bags, they had their med kits on their backs, and they were out the door the next day, conducting liaison and setting up clinics and things like that.

# 3

# BASE

Life on a foreign Canadian Forces base tends to vary with the mission: on some, the soldiers have all their needs taken care of, but on others they deal with Spartan facilities and difficult conditions.

For some soldiers, the base is almost all they see during their mission; for other soldiers, the base is a necessary but boring break from their work in the field. But all Canadian soldiers take immense pride in their temporary homes. They ensure they have the best amenities, and they expend every possible effort to ensure their bases are safe, secure, clean, and well-maintained.

## Afghanistan, 2006-07

Canada House was the big Canadian building there. It had a little store, and it had the big screen TVs with the hockey games on. They had a certain schedule that they got fed from Ottawa. You got the CBC news, then you got the hockey games, the Super Bowl, the big football games, you got it all there. It was a nice place to go when you're in camp.

We'd come into the main camp for 48 hours at a time. You shared a room, but you shared it with another guy in a different troop, so you were never in the room at the same time. Really that was all the time you wanted because you'd come in, you'd go to the PX, eat properly, shower, do whatever you needed to do in your room. But by that time you were so bored you wanted to go back out because the time went so slowly when you were in camp.

## Cyprus, 1991

We had everything. The Internet wasn't the big thing then, but we had videos upon videos, VCRs, TVs. We'd rotate the videos through the different platoon houses every week. As long as you weren't on duty you were allowed to go out for drinks.

We had air conditioning. We had bunks or single rooms, depending on your seniority. In the section houses, bunks, but in the platoon house you had your own room. It was a closet, eight feet by ten feet or something. It wasn't that big, but it was enough for sleeping and to get some time alone, and you had your own private desk where you could write your letters. So the accommodations were pretty good.

## Haiti, 1995-96

We were living in tents; there was no hard accommodation. We were in big modular tents with white camouflage on top to deflect the heat. That was our accommodation at the airport for six months.

The base was extremely clean. We had porta-potties; they were emptied every day, cleaned every day, disinfected every day. Our streets were always swept clean. We were very conscientious, the people on the base, not to throw paper, cigarette butts, nothing. We had to live on the base with rats, spiders, tarantulas, so it was nothing to lift the platform and find 40, 50 families of spiders, tarantulas, underneath your tent, or even to have a spider on your bed in the middle of the night.

Now our beds, we made them ourselves. It was nothing that was brought from Canada, no springs, mattress, pillow, blanket, no such thing. We had four-by-fours for the legs, and plywood with a little sponge on it, and we had our sleeping bag for a blanket. Then we had a mosquito net wrapped around that bed so that we don't have mosquitoes, the big thing was malaria there. The Canadians always had the malaria pills every week at the same time, same day. If you didn't take it, too bad, you get malaria. If you've never heard the symptoms of malaria, malaria is like a very bad flu but instead of lasting 24 hours it will last for weeks. Very high fevers, loss of control of your body and everything.

There was a lot of sunstroke and things like that. There was a little hospital there, an American hospital. If you had sunstroke or were dehydrated and you went to the hospital, they put you in a bed, they pumped fluids into you, a litre or two, and then you felt like a million dollars, and the doctor would tell you, drink more water. The little things, headaches, scrapes, nothing serious.

However, sometimes something serious happened, like when we had six Canadians involved in an accident. They were taken away from Haiti to a hospital in Miami and then back to Canada. So we had a little hospital in the camp, but nothing to keep a guy in for a week, two weeks, just minor things. We had a doctor in there, nurses in there, and if it was anything serious like malaria, which we didn't have too many cases of, they took them to the American hospital, which was air-conditioned and all that. They were only modular hospitals. No solid foundations.

We were very careful in what we did. Myself, I bite my fingernails a lot. When I went to Haiti I learned not to bite my fingernails because you are shaking hands with the people out there and most of them don't have water to wash their hands. We always carried gloves with us. We had wet naps that we used to carry to clean our hands all the time. And every time you came to the base for lunch the first thing that came to your mind was wash your hands so before you go eat; you went to the sink and cleaned yourself. Infections were the most dangerous thing. If you get a cut you right away put something on it, or went to the hospital and took care of it, didn't let it stay exposed to the elements.

## Cambodia, 1994

Our camp was right across the road from the airport, so it wasn't like we were really remote. The camp was the pride of the fleet. I mean, we had militaries from all over the country come to see it. By the end of our tour, there was a UN soccer league set up. Countries with contingents from all over Cambodia would come to our camp to play soccer because we had made such a beautiful soccer pitch. The conditions on the camp were very much First World. We were probably as good as any camp in an established UN theatre.

We were crammed in really tight. When the first Canadians hit that camp, there was this great long building, a good 75 to a 100 yards long, probably 15 to 20 yards wide. We were told that it had been an old driving school, back before the killing fields days, and when the first troops from Petawawa got there it was knee-deep in water and there were water buffaloes in there. So they chased them all out and pumped the water out, fixed the holes in the roof, and generally made it more inhabitable.

So when we got there the roof was good, they'd poured

a concrete floor, but you've still got a 180 guys sleeping in there. So your little corner of the world was probably about six feet wide by seven feet long; as long as your bed and as wide as your bed, plus your shoulders, plus your locker.

Because of the bugs, we had to sleep under mosquito netting all the time, leave our boots upside down and shake them out before putting them on. At one point, some company in Montreal donated air conditioning, so we got eight or ten huge industrial air conditioning units shipped over to Cambodia for our barracks. We had to use a lot of ingenuity just to make the air conditioning work, because the building was not sealed at all, so you'd be pumping in air and it would just flow outside. We ended up sealing the whole building with black plastic, except for the doorways. So we were comfortable that way.

Another company donated an above-ground swimming pool. We had a three million dollar reverse-osmosis water purification unit—you could basically take a crap in one end of it and drink what came out the other end. It was that good.

I would have to say that, looking today at how some of the guys have to live in the forward operating areas in Afghanistan, I'm almost ashamed at the way we lived in Cambodia. When we were out in the jungle it was a different story, but on the base in Phnom Penh, we had it very good. We were really fortunate.

# Central African Republic, 1998

In Africa we actually had hard accommodations because the French were there for many years. We were in a French base and actually we had air conditioning in our rooms. However, it was much hotter in Africa, I believe it was mostly 50 degrees. It was more jungle-like. You find it hard, yes, but you manage.

It was hard in Africa. You had to fight the heat, you had to fight the malaria. The food was not as great because we were eating from the mess hall of the French base, so we had French people making our meals, no Canadian cooks.

# Qatar, 1990

Initially Canada Dry 1 was the only camp in Qatar. The name was given to the camp because there were no alcoholic beverages allowed in the camp. The folks back home thought we had named it after them, so the Canada Dry company back in Canada was sending us all kinds of beverages free of charge. Of course, we never did tell them, we just kept accepting their kind gifts.

We searched out a location where we could set up a camp, and this camp became known as Canada Dry 1. When we first saw Canada Dry 1, it was a terrible shock. It was filthy. There was a cinder block wall around the compound, which of course wouldn't have stopped a Volkswagen if he decided to run into it. The Royal Canadian Regiment came in and set up and they immediately began fortifying the area. They put up machine gun posts all around the perimeter inside the wall.

There were no air conditioners in the rooms or in the buildings, and there were anywhere from 24 to 50 people in a room. Some of the rooms were quite large, and the smaller rooms had 24 in them. You take a room about the size of your average bedroom at home, and you could have up to 20 people sleeping in it, in bunk beds two and three high. Very close quarters.

The ablution areas were absolutely filthy when we arrived. We had to scrape the kitchen area with a putty knife to get the grease off the wall. Very, very dirty. The migrants who were living there were of Mideast descent, and their cooking method involved a lot of grease. They didn't bother cleaning up the spatters, which after several years had accumulated on the wall. I promise you, it was at least a half-inch thick.

In the cleaning process, the folks decided that not only were they going to clean the place up but they were going to beautify it. They started painting murals on the walls, and some of them were exceptional. I wish I'd taken pictures of them, because they were really beautiful. 409 Squadron had, I think, the best. They were the air force squadron that was attached to us in support of the CF-18s.

I think we were very safe where we were, especially with the RCR (Royal Canadian Regiment). They were there 24 and 7, all the time, walking the walls in constant vigilance. I have to take my hat off to those guys. They were exceptionally hard-working in maintaining the security. Even if there wasn't anybody that came at us, the outside world could see that we were vigilant and prepared in case they did so. It was very reassuring to us who were inside these walls.

# Rwanda, 1994-95

I was already in my 50's, but thank god I was in quite good physical shape. I lost a lot of pounds, 15 pounds if not more while I was there, because it was go go go all the time. This tension was building up all the time, from morning till night, seven days a week, you don't stop on Sunday there, it's seven days a week.

Each one of us was given a box of army rations, plus a bottle of water, per day. When I arrived there they put me in a room with my two buddies from Mogadishu that had come there with me. But there was no bed, absolutely nothing, because all of this was UN offices before the war. When the war broke out, many of the UN people were evacuated, civilians and some military as well, so many of those offices were left empty. All of the UN people from General Dallaire down could never go back to their houses where they were living before the war.

After the war started everybody had to sleep and work and eat in the UN building. So my two buddies and myself ended up in an empty office. And for the first two or three weeks there we just slept on the floor with our sleeping bags. After that we managed to get some little army beds. Forget about pillow and sheets, but it was not so bad.

The building used to be an old hotel, so each room had a toilet and a little sink but no running water. In order to use the toilet and shave, with no running water, you could use only whatever water you could find in some little creeks. Wherever you could find it. One of the three of us had to fill up two or three jerry cans of water each day, and with this water we had to wash our clothes, wash the floor of our room because it was the rainy season and everything was very muddy outside, and the rest we would use in the toilet. Those living conditions are not too good, I can guarantee you that.

There was no shower there at all. You just wash yourself. You can't imagine when you have been walking amongst dead people all day, you come back and the smell you feel has gotten into your clothes, your skin, and you cannot take a shower. You cannot even wash yourself properly. It was terrible.

I remember one day it started to rain heavily. Although we were forbidden from doing it, I climbed onto the roof of the building, and I had some soap with me and a towel and I stripped down naked and I said rain, baby, rain! And I washed myself and I could not care less if bullets or bombs were flying. I said, today I'm gonna have a shower. And I did. The General would not have been happy because you were supposed to be more careful than that. But that day I said I'm going to have a shower, that's it.

## Kosovo, 1999

The things we missed were things like flushable toilets. Or just running water. All we had was bottled water, and we were only entitled to so much water per day and you had to really manage your water correctly. The last thing you're gonna do is waste your water for brushing your teeth. Simple things like that, little things.

Because we are the best fed army in the world, so really you get your three meals a day, and then snacks the cooks make. You don't go hungry. You have a place to sleep that keeps you dry. Not as warm, but dry. So you still have your basic amenities, it's just the nicer ones you have in Canada that you miss.

## Afghanistan, 2003

When we arrived we were living in modular tents, but we were only living in those for six weeks; by September we moved into Weatherhaven tents. The battle group arrived a little bit later to take over security, and they moved straight into the Weatherhaven tents and they started conducting operations as soon as possible.

What the battle group knew was Camp Julian, and most people were saying, I've never seen a Roto 0 before like this, even in Bosnia. To the military detriment and benefit, it certainly gave the soldiers a different impression of what a Roto 0 should be like in the future. Regardless of the amount of hardship or risk you give them, they will still expect a higher standard of amenity and accommodation than they previously were given.

For the most part, things were up and running when the soldiers came in. It had a completely outfitted gym, it had the messes all set up, and it had a Can-Ex there. Some of them in limited service—some of the gym facilities were still being created. They hadn't created the little outdoor gym just yet, so the soldiers could work out in the sun. There were initial services already in place, particularly important things like the travel people who arrange all of the flights, the laundry facility, and the welfare phones. They expanded after a while, the number of computers and stuff increased, but basics were in right away, so the soldiers moved into a very comfortable operating picture.

## Cambodia, 1993-94

The camp we were at was on the outskirts of Phnom Penh. It actually used to be a CPAF (Cambodian People's Armed Forces) transport school. We were the second rotation there; the first was from (CFB) Valcartier, and they had already set up the camp. That's basically all the first rotation did, was build the camp, because the city of Phnom Penh had actually been liquidated by that point, so people were just starting to move in as the UN showed up. They actually found dead animal carcasses in the barracks when they got there.

The barracks was just a hut. It was about 200 metres long, with partition walls for each platoon, and each platoon had about four sections' worth of guys. So basically it was one building for about 250 people, partitioned four ways, with our quarters at one end.

We had one of the biggest camps, so we had our own

soccer field, our own gym, we brought a pool, an above-ground pool—we were really popular with the other countries. We were right at the airport, just on the outskirts of town, so we had the Australians to our left and the Polish to our right, we had Ghanans in front of us—this sounds like a bad poem.

The dust was disgusting. It was clay, and you just got caked in it. Sometimes your hotel had water, and sometimes it didn't, so it was pretty funky.

## Qatar, 1990

We had a large vehicle driven by an Arab that used to come in and take the slops away, from the kitchen and from the washroom. He'd pump the main tanks out into this big vehicle, like a big septic tank. At the gate, there were a series of bumps that the vehicles had to go over so that nobody could come racing in, they would get bottomed out if they tried to rush through the area. And this truck had a lid on the top that could be closed and sealed to prevent slops from spilling out of the top.

On this one particular day, the driver forgot to seal it. There was a guard standing at the gate, waiting for him to come out, and he hit the first bump and of course the slop came splashing out all over the poor guard. It was quite a mess. He ended up staying on duty for the next two hours in that condition, because he didn't have anybody to replace him, and not too many people would go near him. When he got back to the quarters he had a bit of extra room all to himself.

## Cambodia, 1994

There were snakes and scorpions living in the barracks, king cobras, and boas and various other types of snakes that would live under the sea containers and on the barracks. We caught a king cobra. He was the better part of six feet long, and we caught him in this cage.

The whole idea of trying to catch a lot of these animals was to get them back to Canada to show people that this was the stuff we were operating with. This is what a scorpion looks like, this is what a rhinoceros beetle looks like. We didn't have any of that for pre-training for the troops because nobody had been in that climate before.

Whenever we'd catch or kill anything like that, we'd try to preserve it as much as possible—put it in formaldehyde or whatever. So we catch this king cobra. But it's in a cage, and it's alive, and no one wants to get too close to it because they can spit their venom. They've got a little pocket in the bottom of their mouths to spit their venom, and if you get it in your eye, it's just as if they bit you and it'll kill you just as quick. We put a blanket over the cage because we figure it'll stop him from spitting.

You had to be there to get the gravity of the situation. Here you've got a bunch of grown men, sitting around trying to figure out the best way to kill this snake. We don't want to shoot it because we're trying to preserve the integrity of the snake. We don't want to damage it in any way.

So we figure who would better know what to do with this snake than the locals? Outside the main gate of our base, there were always locals in taxis, sitting outside our camp to take troops into town. We figure they should know what to do with this thing.

We take it out there and the first thing they wanted to do was take it home and eat it, but we told them they couldn't have it. We just needed to kill it. This one guy takes one of our combat bootlaces and makes a noose out of it, sticks it through the top of the cage, puts it around the snake's neck and pulls it right up against the top of the cage so now it can't spit because it can't breathe. He ties it off to the top of the cage.

We had these barricades at the front gate, which were oil drums, half-filled with cement to stop charging trucks. It had been raining, so the tops of the drums were filled with water. So we put the cage into the water to drown the snake now. Half an hour later, we come back, take the cage out, the snake is limp; everything is good. Untie the snake, take it out, walk it into the camp into the little mess area, showing off this snake, and everybody's taking trophy pictures.

Then it was time to take him into the medical area and put him in a thing of formaldehyde that the doctors had come up with. Once we were in this confined little room with about four guys, we realize the snake is not dead. As we go to put the snake in the formaldehyde, it must have been the formaldehyde that made him wake up. He flipped.

Of course, the guy that was holding him let him go. Now we've got a six foot king cobra loose on the floor in probably a 150 square foot room, with four or five grown men screaming like school girls, dancing around trying to make sure the snake doesn't get a hold of them. To be honest, I can't even remember how we resolved that. I believe he ended up getting danced on so badly he died and we just threw him in the formaldehyde.

The crickets were the size of your thumb. You only saw them once in eight months and they came in for three days. They covered everything. You couldn't walk on the floor because it was covered in crickets. Then they were gone as quickly as they came. The kids would have empty pop bottles and they'd run around and grab these crickets and stuff them in the pop bottles and then sell them to people as food.

## Somalia, 1994

It was difficult, but the working conditions were 100% better than when I got to Rwanda. It was dangerous in Somalia but in Somalia we were all living in air-conditioned trailers, not always but sometimes air conditioned vehicles, and the office was air-conditioned, the kitchen where we used to eat was air-conditioned, so at least we had some of these advantages.

I was sleeping in a trailer and it was reasonably comfortable, taking into account that outside was about anywhere between 40 and 45 degrees Celsius. But of course we didn't go out at night for beer or anything; you were confined to one compound which was guarded by Pakistani soldiers armed to the teeth, and that's how we lived.

# Afghanistan, 2006-07

We built this bunker in our FOB (Forward Operating Base). It was literally 117 feet long, and it was a big accomplishment. It was massive, 500-pound beams that we had to move in by hand. We got it finished on Christmas Eve and moved in, so we had a home for Christmas. Just our troop. The other guys had been there ahead, and they built a small one for each detachment. We built a huge one for all 37 of us. It was cool. When we moved in there we were so happy, because it was Christmas Eve and we had a roof.

Those little things made it bearable. We had to sandbag it, we figured at least 15,000 sandbags through the whole thing, and most of them were filled by us. Then we got the Afghani workers filling sandbags for five bucks a day. It was funny because the engineers came and gave us the idea, but it was all trial and error on our part. We put it all together with people's different levels of expertise. That was one of our pastimes. The giant bunker.

# Golan Heights, 1999

It was pretty much what we expected in terms of what it looked like because one thing they did in preparation was have people who had been there, who were able to show pictures of what the place looked like. That's always a bit of a comforting factor to see when you arrive that yes, it is what I was told it was going to be like.

Living conditions were excellent. We had buildings in Camp Ziouani that were quartered into rooms and stuff and they were air-conditioned. The bunker that I worked in on a regular basis was obviously cooler because it was a bunker, and it was air-conditioned. The searing heat I only had to endure walking around the camp and then travelling around in the area by vehicle. We did regular tours of the area by vehicle patrol. We didn't want to have to have our trucker report back to us that this road is blocked, or that all of sudden the Syrians won't allow us down this route or something like that, so we patrolled.

# Sri Lanka, 2005

We landed there on New Year's Day, and the tsunami happened Boxing Day, so we were in theatre in less than a week. We had to have a camp that wouldn't negatively impact on the disaster area. You don't want to set up a camp in the disaster area and suck up all the resources—"Oh, by the way, we're going to buy up all the food."

I was very conscious as the company officer to place the camp location outside of the disaster area, close to where we could deal with the local government, but also close enough to drive to any of the affected areas, not just one part of the area. While the Red Cross was in one area and could deal locally there, we had mobile teams that could deal with the whole affected area.

CIDA's (Canadian International Development Agency) speed with making that massive logistic undertaking actually happen, saw to it that in a day or two of our medical people arriving in our camp, they were out there delivering humanitarian aid—much quicker than a lot of NGOs (Non-Governmental Organizations) were able to get into the theatre and set up. They may have been in the theatre quicker but they weren't set up and providing aid as fast as we were.

# DAY-TO-DAY

The day-to-day life of a peacekeeper is intense, difficult, and often dangerous. The working environment, living conditions, and amenities are never what the soldier is used to, in the privileged Canadian lifestyle.

Canadian soldiers, however, have always taken pride in adapting well to their surroundings, and finding ways to cope with the boredom, tension, and the different world they confront every day while overseas.

# Cambodia, 1993-94

The mission was about stabilization and democracy. The Khmer Rouge were pushed into a corner. The Vietnamese were responsible for liberating most of the country, but even the Vietnamese gave up and walked out of the country, so here's the Khmer Rouge all backed up. They were actually fighting; they weren't keeping to themselves. There was always fighting, way up north. So we were just there to set up for the first democratic elections in a long time.

Day to day life depended on what your unit's rotation was. I think it was two weeks' driving followed by one week of general duties. So you could either be going out in the local area where you'd be driving out in the morning, fight across the worst traffic in the universe for the day, picking stuff up for the camp or dropping stuff off here and there. Or you could be driving as far as the Thai border, up in Battambang.

You'd wake up four or five in the morning, go do your PT (Physical Training), go grab brekkie, go DI (Driver Inspection) your vehicle, and then hop out and do your drive. If you were doing long distance you had to really prepare. There was a checkpoint on the way to Battambang, a brick tower with a .50 cal (machine gun) on the roof. Everyone stopped to get your picture taken with the guys, and have your picture taken with the machine gun.

And then you'd drive up and hit Battambang, and when you got there you'd always have an overnight. Even though the travel distance, I don't even think it was 200 kilometres, but it took you the better part of ten hours to get there. The roads were in a nasty, nasty state. So it was absolutely horrible, the driving conditions. You'd get up there and drop your load or pick up your load that night.

So you'd do that for two weeks, and then your third week was usually spent on local defence. Really, we weren't a high security concern until towards the end. There were just two guys on picket at night; you did your little walk around, and that was it. When you were on the base platoon, you were local defence, or you were the lawnmower guys.

The hardest thing was driving for eight hours in vehicles without radios, and even if they had radios it didn't matter because the country didn't have any radio stations. You'd try to wear your Walkman, but you had to be careful in case there was any noise you had to worry about that.

# Haiti, 1995-96

My job was to gather intelligence for the Canadian Force Commander in Haiti. While I was there some of my duties were to gather information, and once a week to count all the prisoners in the jail in Haiti, which was in Port-au-Prince, the federal penitentiary.

In Haiti, even today, there is no infrastructure left. The police force is very unprofessional, no experience, no education. So we were counting prisoners. Another thing we were doing was counting dead bodies at the morgue. We used to go to the morgue once a week or two weeks and count how many bodies were there. They were all tagged and everybody that was not claimed by family, they threw them out. They were put in a truck and buried in a mass grave. The UN in collaboration with the Haitians were doing that.

We were involved in quite a few uprisings in the city, like strikes. We had to get in the middle of the strike there to find out why was the strike happening, and what the strike could do to the country. We had about 600 Canadian troops there and if something were to flare up we had to know. We also had the Canadian embassy there, and we were providing information to them.

It was extremely hot, the country, third world country, which I believe is one of the worst ones on this earth, even today.

A lot of poverty, a lot of smells, because garbage was not picked up. Cars abandoned in the streets all over the place. You see vehicles over there that there's no way you'll see here, even in a car derby. The frames are all crooked so on the street you think they're coming at you but they're actually going straight, because the frames are so crooked.

The Force Commander recommended that Canadian troops not go out at night unless they were in armoured vehicles with helmets and flak jackets. You could hear the gunfire everywhere. It was not unusual to see dead bodies on the street at any given time. If there is a dead body nobody touches it until the justice of the peace goes over there and actually declares him dead. No investigation is done, the police sometimes are not even called. The dead body is given over to family, or thrown in the morgue and tagged.

Most of the time we were spending about 16 hours, between 12 and 16 hours, on the streets. We also spent time at the UN headquarters, where we did all our reports. Our routine was, we were get up at five o'clock every morning, get a shower, shave, go eat breakfast, then go to the UN headquarters and be briefed about what had happened during the night. Then we went in town in accordance with the debrief to get information. Then around one o'clock in the afternoon we used to go back to the camp again and eat lunch because you couldn't eat in the streets. The food that they had in the streets was contaminated. It was okay for them but not for us. Many times we missed lunch because we couldn't be there in time.

After lunch we used to go back to the UN headquarters for five minutes to replenish, get water or whatever, and then take up again on the streets and come back for suppertime. Many times after supper we had to go back on the streets or back to the UN headquarters to do the reports so we can submit it to the Force Commander for the next day. That was basically our routine six days a week.

# Rwanda, 1994-95

My full time job was being UN spokesperson. Shortly after I arrived, no aircraft came to Rwanda at all, except one Canadian C-130 Hercules that came once a week. That aircraft was coming from Nairobi, and it would carry our food, our water—no beer, I can guarantee that—one bottle of water per day per man. One. And one box of German army rations, containing three meals, per day. For field rations they are not the best. Sometimes I used to think they were outdated.

I started as UN spokesman when there was only one aircraft coming to Kigali, one aircraft per week. There was no way that a journalist could come to Rwanda at that time except coming through the airport. The journalists were cameramen, writers, photographers, and big players, CBC, BBC, CNN, from all over the world in fact, press agencies, writers, AFP, from France, AP, Canadian Press. They would gather in Nairobi to get on that Canadian aircraft. But in that Canadian aircraft there were only so many seats, because that aircraft had to bring the food and water for us. Each week I was allotted so many seats for the journalists.

I had a list that was forwarded to me from Nairobi of the journalists that were waiting there to come. Totally arbitrarily, I would select them. Throughout the war, I managed who was to come to Kigali and who was to go back. If a guy wanted to stay for a month, but there were people waiting to come, I would touch him on the shoulder and say, my friend, I'm sorry but tomorrow on the aircraft you have to go because somebody else wants to come.

There was another big problem with having too many journalists in Kigali. Although we wanted to have as many as possible, we had to feed these people, to give them water, and to give them a bed someplace. That was also my responsibility, and their security too.

There was no way that anybody could travel in Kigali or in Rwanda except in a UN vehicle. In civilian vehicles, you were shot at immediately, you were going to get killed in a matter of minutes. I had been given two little minibuses, plus I have my own

4x4, so my two little vans with two UN officers and two drivers, we would drive the journalists from point A to point B. That's the only way they could travel.

Every morning there was the commander's meeting at seven o'clock, and there I would learn the general situation of the war, who was where, what was going on. Then I would go back to my other room with the journalists and hold a press conference every day. Just a normal sort of a press conference, but nobody ever interfered with what I was telling the journalists. Nobody said I was telling them too much or not telling them enough. This was my judgement.

I would tell them yes, this happened, this happened, then the press corps would decide amongst themselves where they wanted to go. Let's say there had been a major battle, a massacre, you name it, something that they would think was interesting for them near the airport. Maybe a group of seven or eight would say, well, we want to go to the airport. Another group would say no, we'd rather go to the hospital because there had been this battle, however many civilians massacred had been transported there.

Wherever they wanted to go, I had to assess the danger of going there, and if I thought it was too dangerous to go to one of the places, I would say there, we cannot go. We were travelling in what we call light-skinned vehicles, just a normal 4x4 or minibus. One bullet hole can make a lot of damage. So sometimes the group would be divided into sub-groups, sometimes we would all go together. At the end of the day, they would go back to wherever they were sleeping, before dark, because we would never, never travel when it was after dark, which was about six o'clock at night.

This was probably the greatest challenge of all my life, and I have had some very interesting jobs in my 33-year military career. I had no training whatsoever, I did not even know the difference between somebody from Reuters, or Canadian Press, or AP. From one day to the next I was put right in the middle of that. And it was great. They were very professional press corps people, you did not have the local hometown newspaper there. When you talk about Mike Wallace from 60 Minutes, these are some big people, and of course they all interviewed me, because I was the spokesman.

I received probably the most encouraging comments of all my life from these people. They were telling me, you have no training whatsoever in communication, and we like that, because you tell it as it is.

The relation between myself and the press corps, and literally hundreds went through Kigali, was I would say nothing but excellent. I was very tough with them, strict with them, and they enjoyed it. I ran them just like if they were in the military. If I say you have to be there at seven o'clock, now we are going to this place, and when we get there, you have 20 minutes to do your thing. And in 20 minutes, back into vehicles and we're leaving. And if you're not there, then my friend, you are going to walk back. And they played the game extremely well.

I had a couple of little things with some of them, but they were very rare. If someone didn't want to play the game, I just would leave without talking to them, and that would settle the problem very quickly. After the press conference they ask questions of course, and then the senior people would try to catch me on the side, and they'd say you said this and this and this, but come on, give me a little more, so that they have a quote or something that they can write an article on. So of course I would play the game, too. I'd, you know, come up with something.

But if someone had misquoted me, which happened a couple of times, I would say my friend, if you do that again, you know... This happened very rarely. One journalist one time had misquoted me and that got me into a lot of trouble with the UN Human Rights organization. The journalist, a guy from Reuters of London, was kind enough to write an official statement apologizing and saying yes, he misquoted me, and that relieved me of the trouble. So to make a long story short my relations were extremely good.

It was so good that some journalists wrote books about their experiences in Rwanda and other places and one of them, John Steele, a Reuters cameraman, wrote a book a few years ago about his experiences around the world, including one chapter on Rwanda. In this chapter he uses my name, without exaggeration, about three times on each page. So I thought this was very kind of him and at the same time I think it showed the relationship I had with those people.

## Qatar, 1990

We had just over 200 people in our particular group. We were there from September 15th to December 4th, just prior to the actual outbreak of war. We were doing all the setup, and we were there because war was expected to break out at any time. My particular job as a sergeant-major was the dress and deportment and looking after the soldiers and airpersons that we had on the base. Anything that the air force, the flyboys as we called them, wanted, that's what we did.

The work there was intense, very hard, back-breaking work. Although we were told we were going to be in the desert, the desert in that area was hard. It was like limestone or sandstone, very difficult to dig, and we had to fill thousands and thousands of sandbags. I have to say, the RCR did an exceptional job. The other troops chipped in to help them, including some of the air force personnel from 409 Squadron. They actually had competitions to see how many sandbags they could fill in their given volunteer time. They would go down there for two hours, for example, and there would be quite a competition to see if they could fill more sandbags than the team that was on before them, or the team that would be on the next night.

The RCR also took very large metal 45-gallon drums, cut the tops off, and filled them with rock for exterior protection. This was prior to the time when we got the big blocks of cement, which formed the barrier around the outside to prevent any car bombs from driving directly in on us.

## Afghanistan, 2003

I had the fun job of being the senior visit officer, coordinating and running the visits for all of the senior people. 18 VIP visits happened in the six months I was there, including the Prime

Minister, the Governor General, and Rick Mercer's "Christmas in Kabul" tour—I wasn't bored.

I had to handle things like the senior NATO representative from Brussels who came over there, the CLF (Commander, Land Forces), General Hillier, who was going to become the next ISAF commander, the Chief of the Air Force. I wouldn't call it military tourism because obviously most of those people were there to take back valuable lessons to improve their own organizations, to be able to support the mission.

Morale was buoyed by a visit from the CDS (Chief of Defence Staff) at the time, and certainly the visit by the Governor General. It wasn't just a photo op; Governor General Clarkson very much boosted the moral of the soldiers going there. So did Rick Mercer, and the visit of Tiger Williams and the other hockey players.

General Leslie made no bones about it, he wanted to encourage people to come to Afghanistan, to see what we were doing, to see the progress we were making, to see the kind of environment we were living in. A lot of people thought he was trying to gain personal accolades that way, but I don't believe that, because I was the one setting up the schedules of what these people did and General Leslie was very specific to me in what these people needed to see.

It wasn't just sitting down and having a warm fuzzy talk with him about what the mission needed. He tried to get people out there to see as many of the different organizations within ISAF and the Canadian locations, as much as could be done safely, to make sure that they had a true perspective of what Canadians were accomplishing, and the kind of jobs and the environment that they were operating in.

We were responsible as the military in the theatre for the safety of all Canadians in the theatre. I was involved in developing a Non-combatant Emergency Evacuation Plan, to cover every Canadian that was operating in Afghanistan, like people with aid organizations. That became difficult because Canadians with some aid organizations didn't register with the Canadian embassy when they arrived, so no one knew exactly how many Canadians were in Afghanistan, where they were operating, or how best to contact them.

There were a number of things we did. We said to our contacts in different organizations, get us a list, tell us the names of the Canadians working with you. We then went to the more interesting approach of organizing Canadian gatherings at our camp, Camp Julian. We had a Canadian Barbeque in Camp Julian to welcome all Canadians. Of course there had to be a guest list for all of these people, and they had to have their identity confirmed at the gate before we let them in.

We screened the Canadians when they arrived and said oh, who do you belong to, sort of gathering info. And in case we need to get hold of you in the future for more of these, what's your e-mail address? So we were actually able to get a pretty good database, just by doing the social scene. All these Canadians came out of the woodwork as soon as they hear about a Canadian beer and steak party. We weren't the only people doing that kind of thing, but it worked very well.

## Bosnia, 1996

The headquarters was in downtown Zagreb, and we were actually accommodated  in an old military barracks out at the Zagreb International Airport. I would be at the headquarters by 7:30 in the morning. There would be an operational briefing for the force commander, I'd sit in on that every morning. Following that I normally had a meeting with the Force Commander where we talked about any ongoing issues or problems that had to be addressed, what we were going to do during the day.

We did travel a fair bit. Of course, when he was on the road I had to be in the headquarters, and he was out and about quite a lot. Then there were meetings. The Secretary-General's special representative would have a weekly meeting, sometimes twice weekly meeting, and for a while that was Kofi Annan. I worked with him as a Secretary-General's Special Representative. He had come out of being the Director of Peacekeeping in New York and went back to become the Secretary-General of the UN.

Once a week, I got together with all the non-governmental

organizations and we gave them a briefing on the military situation, talked about some of the troubles and difficulties they were having and how we might be able to facilitate delivery of humanitarian aid or peace, refugee issues, and so on.

## Former Yugoslavia, 1992

In a lot of combat situations like that, the RCMP were involved. They were sent over there to help the local police get established and maintain control. Their job was extremely hazardous; they had a rough time over there. Not only was it hazardous, but also they didn't have the protective equipment we had. We had flak jackets and steel helmets, and they had nothing. They went over there in just their ordinary day clothes.

They were about 30 kilometres south of us, in a town that had been totally bombed out and was just starting to rebuild. Quite a large place. They came to us and asked for advice about the bombs and munitions and what they needed to know. We gave them the briefing, and also gave them flak jackets and steel helmets. And when their boss came over to visit, he made them give it all back! I said, well this is stupid, and got them to take it back again the day after he left.

They did some amazing work over there, just phenomenal. One of the biggest problems was that the police force over there was just totally corrupt. They had to fight through that and gain the trust of the local population, and they did that exceptionally well.

The RCMP guys joined our sergeant's mess up there. They were like us; they would come in there and just get totally blitzed and release, get in a fight, throw a couple of hundred sandbags at somebody or something. There were all kinds of ways of relieving the tension and the pressure.

## Afghanistan, 2006-07

Our final FOB had the ANA (Afghan National Army) right there. We didn't work with them, the Americans had different groups that worked with the ANA, not us. But we got to interact with them. We showed them how to clean their weapons; their weapons were filthy, rusty. We had to show them how to grease them. They would sit there and pop rounds all night, indiscriminately, whenever they felt like it. Bang, ba-bang! The new guys came to replace us, and they just freaked when the guys started popping rounds, they dived for cover, but we were used to it.

You'd just be walking across the gun position and they'd fire a rocket or something. They did it almost every day. Someone fired an RPG by accident in the building. Another shot his buddy in the chest, he had to be airlifted out. He may or may not have made it. We never found out the final details. He went out on the chopper so you never find out. They would walk around, fiddling with their radios to get the Top 40, the Afghani Top 40 or whatever it was.

## Golan Heights, 1999

It was an easy mission compared to what some of the guys had gone through in the initial tours with the UN in '91, '92. But the problem was most of the people in the Golan Heights were not combat arms people. We had the occasional one, there were certain people from combat arms, only to make sure that there was a standard set for all of the logistics people.

I'll be honest, we had some pretty frightening people who came with a very serious lack of training. There was a master corporal air force finance type who actually put the magazine in upside down. That was the first time as a combat arms guy when I'd actually seen somebody click in a magazine upside down with the bullets facing down in a C7 rifle. I didn't think it was possible but it was proven to us that it was. These are the kind of people we were going to give weapons to and live ammunition to as gate guards. Nothing that would be like what the guys dealt with in Bosnia that way, but this was as close to Bosnia as a lot of the logistics people would ever come.

A lot of these people certainly had misguided understanding of what they would be employed at. There were a lot of clerks who thought, "My job is going to the finance office every day from eight to four, I'll have weekends off and I don't need to carry a weapon or anything like that, why do I need to have all this training?" without sort of realizing the full operational picture. They had been told by previous groups, you'll be doing finance stuff, but you'll be doing it in an air-conditioned office in the Golan. So a lot of them thought it was a Canadian garrison job, just in a different location.

## Bosnia, 2001

I learned about 9/11 via satellite. I was on the gate all night doing camp security. I got off shift about eight o'clock in the morning, so I went to bed. My roommate came in around lunchtime, knocked on my door cause he knew I was sleeping, and he said "I'm going on patrol in a couple hours and I just wanted to let you know we're having hot dogs for lunch. Oh yeah, and some idiot flew a plane into the World Trade Center."

I remember thinking to myself, okay, something for lunch, going on patrol, some idiot flew, what was for lunch again? He said, "No, you didn't hear me." And I said, "Yeah, some idiot, whatever." My attitude was, North America, welcome to the real world. You're now part of what goes on in the world. At that point I'd been in Bosnia for five months, and it was an eye-opener to different peoples' way of life. Here it's normal for people to walk around and see soldiers carrying guns. Back in Canada, people would be calling the cops thinking we're getting invaded. So that was my attitude.

But I got up and I sat and I watched, and then I saw the second plane come in, and, so that was kind of, it was kind of surreal. Two days later they decided oh well, we'd better go on high alert, you were taking your flak vest to the toilet. That only lasted for a day and a half, and then it was back to normal again. But I think you'd find a lot of guys would say the same thing, welcome to the real world.

# 5

# FIELD

The most interesting—and dangerous—part of any mission is the time spent "outside the wire" in the field. In a strange foreign country, where at least some of the locals may be hostile, danger is always present. The field is an unsafe, uncontrollable, high-stress environment.

Depending on their tasks, Canadian soldiers might spend almost all their time on the base, or they might spend most of their time in the field. However, whether the field is a patrol route, a checkpoint, a battle site, or a slum, it is where peace operations really happen.

## Rwanda, 1994-95

The press people don't want to stay in the office, they want to go where the action is. They had to write an article every day and the cameramen had to send pictures every day. Most of them would be there for two weeks, and then they would go back to Nairobi, and then they would be replaced by another crew, sometimes they would come back, some of them came back three times, but no one stayed for the whole time. So whenever I had new people coming in, immediately they wanted to go to the scene of a massacre, although myself I had seen it 15 times.

Many times you still had to cross the front line, where one side was fighting against the other. We have to go through this and after you do that for weeks and weeks, you become less careful. You are inclined to take more chances. The journalists are there for two weeks and they want to make the best of their two weeks, and you try to get the most of their stories and photographs and this and that.

As the guy responsible for the security I had to take that into consideration but at the same time I wanted to help them, because my job was to try to make sure that what was happening, the massacres, the hundreds of thousands of people that were killed per month, that those stories would get out of Rwanda. And the only people that could do that were the press people.

## Cyprus, 1991

Turkey and Greece are separated on Cyprus by a buffer zone, an area through the island from east to west, separating the two countries, maybe 100 metres wide. Basically the UN owned the land. Either country wasn't allowed in unless authorized by the

UN. There were section houses throughout the whole island, where ten or twelve UN guys would stay, rotating in and out with the rest of their platoon.

You had your shift on the tower, and across from you on either side you'd have a Turkish soldier and a Greek soldier in their towers, all spaced out equally. Our job there was to make sure they weren't coming in and at the same time try to maintain the peace.

## Cambodia, 1994

Our whole role there was to provide a convoy support and site security for the elections. The Khmer Rouge had said we're not going to allow the elections to happen, and the UN said, yeah, you are. In the period during the elections, a lot of our guys were divvied up throughout the country in different electoral districts. I was in one of the districts with a private under me.

This was our little corner of the world for approximately 10 days. I think the next Canadians were about a hundred miles away from us. There was us two, two French civilian police that were under the UN auspice, and a contingent, probably about platoon strength, of Indian soldiers. We're in this village, and we're supposed to be staying in this house, the two of us.

We were at this one polling site and we had a translator with us. The people that had come to vote were talking to the translator and he comes to us and says, there's a village about 15 kilometres away from here and the folks can't come and vote because the village is surrounded by Khmer Rouge and there's a couple of village heavies that are basically telling them that they're not allowed to go vote. We took it upon ourselves to decide that, yeah, they're gonna vote. We took our vehicle, which was like a Toyota 4-Runner, a little pick-up truck. We took the translator and the three of us drove out to this village.

There are no roads out there. You're driving on the berms between rice paddies. It is so remote, we get there and everybody is just in awe of this thing that has rolled up because, according to the translator, none of them has ever seen a vehicle. It must be an animal of some kind, because it came in here on its own steam. And then out pops us two enormous guys compared to what they're used to. I mean, a big Cambodian is a hundred pounds. And here these two soldiers pile out of this truck in full battle dress, looking larger than life to them.

Anyway, we had about 22 of them packed into this truck. When we get back to the polling site, we go to the back of the truck and everybody is just dead silent. They look like they got the fear of God in them. And we get them unloaded and tell them where the polling site is and what they have to do obviously through the translator. Once they're in doing their thing, the translator comes up to us and he says there was somebody in the back of the truck telling them who to vote for, and how to vote, and which box to tick off. He was one of these village heavies.

So we called all the people out of the building and lined them up and basically told them again, it's your choice, you can vote for whoever you want and nobody knows who you vote for, and send them back in to do their thing. This heavy, the translator didn't really want to point him out. The translator was scared as well.

Anyway, we start to put these people back in the truck, and one of the ladies was pregnant and she gets in the back of the truck and sits up on the wheel well. This guy comes up to the back of the truck and he grabs her, and he just pulls her off the wheel well, and gets in and sits on it, which may be customary for their culture, but it's not customary where I come from. So I grabbed this guy, I pulled him out of the truck, and I sent him walking. I told the translator, "Tell him he's going to walk back to the village. He's not riding with us." It turns out, he was one of the heavies. Everybody was happy that they didn't have to ride back in the truck with him.

## Haiti, 1995-96

The road conditions were very poor, very little pavement. On the streets a lot of potholes, a lot of garbage, a lot of debris on the street. So it was not uncommon on any given day to change two flat tires on your trucks. You gotta crawl underneath your truck, you're crawling in garbage, you're stepping in garbage. The smell, atrocious smells depending on where you're going in the city, from garbage, from dead bodies.

Because Haiti is on a hillside, with no fences at the bottom, you see all the garbage in the big torrential rains, and they had tropical rains there, all the garbage coming down to the ocean. If you see the ocean from an aircraft at Haiti, Port-au-Prince, one kilometre from the shore it's all muddy. There is no vegetation growing in the ocean, there are no fish, there is nothing. It's all dead because all the garbage drains into the ocean.

That's Port-au-Prince. Traffic, smell, heat, all that combined together for six months. Plus we were driving on unpaved roads for an average of 14 to 16 hours a day. Very hard on the body, very hard on your back and on your spine. That was the hardest part of Haiti.

Information is passed very quickly in that country, even though they don't have phones. The radios, the newspapers, it takes time for the information to go. But word of mouth is passed from one end of the city to the other end in a couple of hours.

Usually when we tried to meet our sources, we tried to tell them where to go, so we see the source coming in, and then we circle and he sees us circle and then we move to another location. From that location we move to another location, he keeps following our truck so nobody sees him coming into the truck with us. And our truck had tinted windows so nobody could see who was in the back.

The main thing for us was to not lose a source. If the gangs found out that they were talking to the UN, that source was dead. So we just finished talking to a source, and were going back to the base for lunch. It took us an hour and a half to get to the base, and when we arrived they told us that one of our sources was dead. We asked which source it was. With our sources we never went by names, we went by numbers, source number 10, source number 15. Source number 20, they said. I was talking an hour and a half ago with that source. That means our source got burnt, not necessarily from that specific day but from other times. But we tried to be very careful not to burn our sources.

We usually asked sources to come over to the UN headquarters to talk to us. Just apply for a job with the UN to clean the camp and things like that and that's where we would meet them. So sources were working in the camp, and every morning we used to debrief the source. When he went home then he knew what happened that night, so he came to the camp in the morning, and then we sat down with him and said okay, tell us what happened last night. That was the best way to protect them.

Some of the sources couldn't work in the camp or didn't want to work in the camp, and we couldn't employ all of those sources, so we had to go meet them in the streets. And sometimes it was up to three, four, five kilometres away, where we had to meet them. If they found that they were at risk, that somebody was following them, they never showed up. Well, I'm sorry, I couldn't go. That's what he'll tell you next time.

So that's how we got our information. Extremely dangerous for them and for us.

# Somalia, 1994

I was in Somalia just a little over three months. Somalia was a war-torn country, unbelievable. It was very dangerous. Some Americans had been killed not too long before, these 10 or 15 Americans, and quite a few Pakistani soldiers had been killed. It was a very dangerous place to be. In fact, I found it, strangely enough, much more dangerous than being in Rwanda, even going through the war. Perhaps because I was not so accustomed to danger. Once I got to Rwanda I was a little bit, I guess. We always travelled in groups, well equipped and well armed, in armoured vehicles all the time. No incidents happened to me or my group while I was there, but it was a difficult place. Terribly hot, 45 degrees.

When I went to Somalia it was night and day compared to my previous tours. The poverty there, and everything in the capital Mogadishu had been totally destroyed, absolutely everything was destroyed in that city. In fact not only in that city, I mean it was terrible.

In addition to my job I was also responsible for visiting the prisons and making recommendations to improve the conditions of the prisoners there, which were absolutely terrible, if you can imagine in a place like that. I used to go from prison to prison when I had time with members of my team and we would talk to the authorities and then look at the prisoners, and write recommendations, trying to help them a little bit.

At that time the US was already in the process of pulling out of Somalia and other countries as well, so the UN wanted to train as best as possible the Somalian police so that when the whole of the UN would pull out, which happened less than a year after I left, you would have sort of a police force and some sort of a justice system.

## Former Yugoslavia, 1992

When we first got to Yugoslavia, we had no idea what the munitions were they were using. We didn't have any mines pro-formas or anything of that nature. Luckily, in a place called Polum, which was up not far from Daruvar, there was a huge munitions factory. We actually stumbled onto it by accident. The gate to the place was closed, it was just a chain link fence, but we could see in, and we could see that the munitions factory had been bombed. There were mines—thousands and thousands of mines, scattered all over the place.

As we were going in, I noticed a wire attached to the fence. I followed it down as it was unusual, it shouldn't have been there. The gate was actually booby-trapped. There were 500 grams of explosives on it. We were able to make it safe and we opened the gate without hurting ourselves. We got inside the camp, now on the lookout for other booby traps, but we never found any others— thank God. I think that must have just been an afterthought as they were closing the gate. Anybody coming along would have had some pretty serious injuries from this pound of explosives around their feet.

Inside this munitions factory, there was absolutely

everything we wanted, in training and in live, and all the fuses to go with it. We took truckloads of this stuff out. We set up all our vehicles with these training mines, anti-personnel mines, anti-tank mines, the whole works. It was quite a find, quite a coup. We also sent seven complete sets back to Canada for the engineer units that were training, so that they would know what the mines in the area looked like. The chaps at home didn't know anything whatsoever, they knew absolutely nothing about what was going on in Yugoslavia. Then we started making up posters and books.

We literally started from the ground up, figuring out how these devices worked. We got on the good side of some Serb engineers, and they explained to us some very fine specifics about how much pressure would be required to set one off, et cetera.

They had a large supply of anti-personnel mines and these were mostly copied from the Russians. There was also what was called the Claymore mine, which was an American mine, a directional mine. But we didn't know that they had these, because these weren't in the factory. The way we found these was actually walking into a Serb minefield and finding them unprotected. We also found that the mines were facing the wrong direction; if fired they would have killed themselves. So, by taking them, we probably saved their lives.

## Cambodia, 1994

Road conditions were unbelievable. You would drive a distance that would be comparable to from Calgary to Edmonton, about 180 miles or 300 kilometres, so about a three-hour drive. And it was a 12 to 15 hour marathon, just because of the conditions of the roads. The roads were so poorly maintained, if you could do 15 clicks, you were moving pretty well. It would shake the vehicles apart.

It was kind of difficult for us there because the Khmer Rouge had already said, "We'll let you move freely during daylight hours. If we catch you on the road after dark, your trucks are ours no matter how we gotta get them from you." So we were mandated that if it's dark out, you go to ground. Obviously you don't want to be going to ground anywhere other than protected territory, of which there was none outside of the camps.

We had to use a little bit of ingenuity on more than one occasion. We had an MLVW (medium transport truck) where a clip inside the axle had broken. The rear wheel on the driver's side had started to come right out of the axle hub. Here we are on the side of the road with eight trucks and we've got one truck with an axle that's coming apart. It's about two o'clock in the afternoon, we've probably got about 30 miles to go to get to camp, and we've still go to fix this vehicle, which is not a lot of time.

So we're trying to decide, are we going to try to salvage this truck? Or are we going to do a denial on it and leave it? We happened to have a couple of mechanics with us on the convoy. What we ended up doing was torching a hole in the bed of the truck, dropping a chain down through the hole, and chaining up around that axle hub to hold it up. We pulled the wheel right out, threw it in the back of the truck, and drove back to the base with five wheels. I've got pictures of that. It was some of the most amazing recovery work that I've seen.

## Bosnia, 2001

We deployed as we would in a combat situation. The HDZ was the Croatian nationalist party. They wanted to separate from Bosnia and join greater Croatia. Which is all part of the history, greater Serbia, greater Croatia, and Bosnia being stuck in the middle. So they wanted to become part of Croatia, but the lines were already drawn according to the Dayton peace accord, so if they separated the Muslims would get in a lot of trouble. So we were enforcing the peace accord, we weren't going to let that happen.

The Croatian side basically stood up to the offensive support group and gave us all these threats, we're gonna do this, we're gonna do that. So we deployed our artillery all throughout Bosnia, just to let everybody know, both belligerents and civilian population, that we were ready. If you want to go through with this, we're ready.

We'd set up in completely obvious places, all along the roads because of the mine threat. That was another thing we had to adjust to, coming over, because we're used to deploying in fields, but it wasn't like that. You'd have a strip of road, and you had to deploy the entire battery on that road. We deployed in both rural and urban areas, just to ensure that everyone got a good look at who we were and what we were prepared to do.

We had authorization to fire from the commander. We were just waiting for the order, which, thank God, never came. It's a real eye-opener when you wake up in the morning and you realize, this could be the day. Being artillery, you're a priority target. You're thinking, this could be the day when I get it. Or one of my good friends gets it. It plays on your mind a bit, but your training kicks in and you're ready to go.

There were two or three weeks where it was really tense. We knew as soon as we got on the ground that the day was coming. There were only two or three weeks of tension, and then later on in the tour it got a little bit tense again, but it's an unstable place, and these things happen.

It's brinkmanship, and it's a dangerous game. But we had all the firepower. They just want to get under your skin and tick you off. They know your rules of engagement, they know exactly what buttons to push, and they do it well. That's what they were doing. So we had to play our game. Unfortunately that took us away from what we were trying to accomplish in framework patrolling and stabilizing the country.

We ramped it up until the date passed, and a couple of days after it passed, the HDZ came out and said, we're going to do it this day in the future. So it was all idle threats but we still had to be prepared. Once NATO was satisfied that it was an idle threat, then we could go back to our peacekeeping, framework patrolling, handing out aid, and stuff like that.

# Afghanistan, 2006-07

There are two guns in each troop. When you go out and set up in the field, you have your CP (Command Post) and two guns, and your four vehicles, and maybe you have medics, and maybe you have a Met truck.

There's 37 dudes and that was all we had. Literally no one else around. Sometimes the other troop would be nearby, but they'd be by themselves. You'd be mutual support and you'd come over to talk to each other, but they could move at any time and we could too. That's how we were in Afghanistan, it was just you and the desert. This is your 37 dudes and 100 by 200 metres or so.

The first month was everything you'd take artillery combat to be. Jets flying overhead, fire missions all night and all day, ammo coming in. We were even running short on some ammo, we fired so much. We were in a warm position.

Some infantry would cycle back to us for a little downtime. It was great because they'd come up and shake your hand, and say, "Thanks, man, you really helped us out." We were firing as little as 300 metres away from our own infantry. It was good that they realized how effective artillery was. They realized that if you employ the artillery before you approach an objective, that objective is a lot easier to take.

They did foot patrols every day but they didn't have enough guys, so they would come to us and we would give them a gunner. So one guy got to leave the guns and go patrol up and down the hills. They had a blast, they loved that. They got to go outside the wire and be infantry guys, walk up and down the mountain. One guy, he didn't want to go outside the wire. And then I found out that he was actually under my command in the FOB, and he was the next guy to go out. Everyone goes out.

I would have gone out too but I couldn't, I had to run the gun. I had a reservist woman on my gun, excellent soldier, huge chip on her shoulder, she went out there on patrol and she ended up going out for one that lasted three or four hours and just covered in sweat by the time, because the elevation is fairly high. She made it, she did pretty well. I was doing six to eight hours sentry myself a day as a sergeant on the line, watching the arcs. So we were spread pretty thin. When guys started going on leave, I was down to five guys at one point, but ten guys is usually what I had.

We'd fire mortar rounds all night, illuminate different routes in, to see if anything happened. We'd also listen to their comm chatter, whatever signals we could pick up from the insurgents talking back and forth. We'd fire into the south and you could hear them talking, they were saying, the rounds are dropping 400 metres behind us, so we'd bring them forward. Then they'd say, oh, they're 100 metres behind us. They'd actually be telling their buddies how close the rounds were and NATO would pick it up and we would fire accordingly. So these guys were actually calling our rounds in on themselves. Crazy stuff.

You'd drive through Kandahar, and these kids would come out as soon as they saw the vehicles to throw rocks. I was at the end of the convoy, and by the time my vehicle came around, I watched a barrage of rocks. Some guys pulled out their pistols and waved them around but I'm not really into that. They're kids. I always got lucky, rocks hit my cupola but I never got hit.

Other kids would come by and they'd wave, and you'd throw candy. We weren't supposed to because the local elders didn't want the kids running out to the trucks. We're massive, eighty-ton vehicles, you don't want kids running towards them. But they'd run anyway. Sometimes you'd drive into a divided highway, and on the divided concrete part one time I saw this little girl. We drove by looking down, and this little girl this big, maybe two? Three? I'm thinking, whose kid is this? Who's leaving their kid in the middle of a divided highway?

You'd see lots of weird things. One disturbing thing we saw was women in burkas—some women you'd see in a burka, some you wouldn't—you'd see some of them crouch down at the side of the road and start grabbing rocks. The guy I was relieving said they were shoving rocks into their areas because they thought we were going to stop and rape them like the Russians. Or they'd been told we were like the Russians. I don't know. They were told rumours that we'd rape them so they'd shove rocks in their areas to stop us from raping them. It was bizarre.

It's sad, you'd drive by and see the kids, and they had growths on their faces from all the bad water. You'd drive over a river, a crappy little river, and these people are washing, these people are getting water. Up the river you can see livestock, people had moved their animals into the water and were washing them. Up the river another guy is washing his dirty, disgusting truck, he's backed it into the river and he's washing it while these people are washing their clothes and getting water downstream. What was he thinking? I don't understand.

A lot of garbage. And the smell. You know, you hit Kandahar, you step out of the camp and you hit the city, and the smell is something you never forget. Supposedly a certain percentage of the dust is feces. There's a sewer system only in certain parts of the city. The smell was awful. So you'd have your goggles on. I had a bandage I used. You'd chew gum and you could taste it in your mouth, just from breathing. As it got colder my driver literally had to wear a full mask with his goggles on; he looked like Darth Vader rolling down the road, waving at the kids and they were waving back.

We had breakdowns, those were annoying. Certain vehicles that weren't very good, they would break down all the time. It once broke down when we were coming through the pass into Kandahar. Coming down through the mountains, it flattened out, and then you come through this range as you come into Kandahar, a mountain range rises up out of nowhere. We're going through there and of course the vehicle dies coming through the mountain range. We had infanteers with us and they were freaking, because we picked the worst spot. You can't go up the mountainside. You can't do anything. But there was an ANP (Afghan National Police) checkpoint on the other side of it, so they went and told them, and as fast as we could, hooked up to another vehicle and towed it.

## Sri Lanka, 2005

As the company commander I would travel around to monitor the progress of our people. We would set up a reverse osmosis site with the engineers in a particular location, and they would build a little camp around it and live at that site. And you could see that growth from a couple of four-man tents set up, with a couple guys watching around it, to basically a little community where the people would come on a regular basis even just to fill up their water jugs and their pop bottles and stuff. But these teams were providing whole containers, tanker trucks of water out to local camps.

I could go to a medical clinic and see the line-up of people there, because you'd picked the right location, people were going to go to it. Or if it wasn't in the right location, you had a mobile team that you could go to another location to do a temporary clinic there, and then say, all right, we'll be back two days from now at the same time, and then move to the next area.

## Cambodia 1993-94

One cool thing about our mission was that you could get attached to the naval reconnaissance group, which was run by the ANZACs, the Australians and New Zealanders. They would take Russian Zodiacs up and down the Mekong and stop in small towns that were right on the waterfront, and get information on troop movement. We went on just one of these trips. Our two boats went up the river, and we stopped at two towns.

The only way in and out of these towns was by boat. We had one major, a Canadian engineer, and he had a sleeve tattoo—his entire arm was just completely covered with ink. And when we went into this town, the locals went retarded because they thought he was a king or something, because tattooing is such an issue with them. They were right freaked out by him. There was also one black Canadian engineer with us, and the kids just went wild, because they'd never seen a black guy before.

The first hour and a half you're in a town is spent just trying to find out who's in charge. First they say, "This guy's in charge." And our major would say, "This guy is way too young to be in charge. Who's really in charge?" And then another guy—well, he might be old enough, but you probe and probe until finally the actual leader, whoever was in charge of the town would finally come out of the crowd and say, yeah, I'm in charge.

Through an interpreter, we would find out information like whether there had been troops in the area, any firefights, any new graves in the area, and that was about it. We spent most of our time just riding around in the boat.

# 6

# DANGER

Easy, safe peace operations are a relic of a past era, if they ever really existed. In the modern world, an element of danger is always present for every Canadian soldier deployed abroad. Snipers, roadside bombs, mines, booby traps, rockets—peacekeepers deal with them constantly. These veterans worked in the midst of all these dangers, and were lucky enough to avoid them and come home safely.

## Former Yugoslavia, 1992

I remember giving an interview one day in the safety of Daruvar. I was in an office, and I was giving a phone interview to a British radio station. There was a window behind me; I was standing with my back to it, and I heard this little tap-tap-tap on the window. I turned around and this guy is pushing an anti-tank mine through the window to me. Here I am, telling the British person about how the kids are forever getting involved on the losing end of the munitions over there, and this guy is passing me an anti-tank mine.

He said, "Here, I just took this away from a group of kids, they were rolling it down the road like a wheel." I grabbed it and the first thing I realized was that it still had its top on, so I unscrewed the lid. The bloody thing was fused! It was ready to go. This guy comes up and just shoves it through the window, here, take care of it.

## Rwanda, 1994-95

There was always the noise of gunfire coming from all around you. Not all the time, I don't want to exaggerate, but many times the odd bomb falling, or sometimes they would start bombing one building in particular, and then if you were too close you'd stop or get out of there.

I was making those kinds of decisions with my other two drivers in the minibuses. We were in contact with walkie-talkies and I had radio communication with the UN headquarters. Sometimes UN headquarters would say, we know you are on the way to the airport, stay away because they are bombing near the airport. So we turn around or change direction or something.

We were coming back from a town called Gitarama, with a cameraman sitting next to me, and two reporters sitting in the back seat, and I say you know this long curve we have to watch it because many times they shoot when we come through here. Not necessarily to get us, but to scare us. And as I was telling him that, he grabbed his camera and put it on his shoulder, just in case something should happen.

Sure enough, as he was doing that they started firing, and on the video, you can hear me screaming on the radio, and see the tracer bullets just in front of my vehicle. You know, that scares you all little bit when you can see the tracers, and you can hear the brrrr of the machine gun. Another vehicle got hit and a couple of guys got seriously injured. But it just so happened that I went through, this is what you call luck.

I don't know how come I was not hit because in the video you can so well see the tracer bullets passing right in front of my car. If some were passing in front, some were passing behind as well, but none hit my vehicle. It was just not my day. This was the time that I remember the most clearly because we have it on film. And it was not cinema, it was the real thing.

I always hated to say that we were deliberately shot at; to my press I would say, no, I don't think they were shooting at us. I would say I think they were shooting at the enemy on the other side of the hill or something like that.

Sometimes you would be traveling on the road, and then sometimes on the left you could hear some small gunfire or hear some bombs starting to fall. You just happened to be close by. They you had to take some measures to get away from there. But mostly the distractions were roadblocks. I would avoid, as much as I could, going into dangerous areas. Because our people were reporting information to us, we knew where the major part of the fighting was going on, and I was not going to drive myself right into the middle of that, at least not intentionally.

We just did not go to many parts of the city, period, regardless of what had happened in those areas. We would try to remain on the main arteries of the city as much as possible. Never mind taking a little shortcut unless you had to, because it was just too dangerous.

At night they would start bombing each other with their artillery. Those bombs would fly over our building or very close over our building, and you can hear the sort of whistle it makes, and then you hear the crash when it has landed not too far away. Our building happened to be for a long time almost right in the middle of the two sides. When they were bombing each other, and they did that at night many times, I guarantee that would wake you up. You'd put your flak jacket on in bed and your helmet and hope for the best. A few times the building was hit.

## Cambodia, 1993-94

We all had our close calls. We had a truck we called Bad Karma, because it got hit three separate times by three separate shooters. It was never aimed at you, it was always just some kid trying to pull you over for cigarettes. They would set up illegal roadblocks, and the rule of thumb was you just put your foot to the floor and leaned on the horn, unless it was something that actually impeded the vehicle. It was usually just a workhorse or something, and you'd just hammer right over it.

Often it was a kid just holding his hand up, so you'd lay on the horn once or twice and you'd hear a pop-pop and a tink, and you'd notice you got a hole in your door or something. You usually didn't find it until you were long gone. More problems from shootings came during national holidays, when the troops were around.

About three-quarters of the way through the trip, the CPAF Army got paid for the first time in two years, and man, they just went on a bender. Even though they'd been paid, they couldn't afford to drink at the nightclubs where the young guys were drinking, so they'd be drinking moonshine or whatever at the local establishment, and we'd hear AKs (AK-47 machine guns) going off, and we'd hide behind trees. They weren't actually aiming at anybody, they were just popping some rounds off.

## Qatar, 1990

During the Gulf War we were tested a few times. Saddam Hussein's Scud missiles were fired at us twice, I believe, but both missed us by a considerable margin. The first time we heard that one had been fired at us, we were actually taking our first day off after 28 days of continuous work, 16 to 18 hours a day minimum. If you were lucky you might get three or four hours of very restless sleep, because of the heat.

## Haiti, 1995-96

I had a partner. We worked as a jeep team, that's what they called it. Basically your partner backs you up. We got into a mob of people. They were going to cut this lady in pieces. We got in the middle of it and it was so intense and so stressful. People were pulling you aside and grabbing you and saying, hey, it's not your business. We're gonna deal with this. And we tried to convince them that hey, there are laws in this country. So there was screaming and pushing and shoving all over the place.

I was surrounded by three or four different people, and I was looking for my partner and I couldn't see him anywhere. I found him in the truck. He was in tears, and he said to me, I cannot do this anymore. A person like that you have to bring back to Canada. Not everyone can cope with that type of stress, confronting a mob people with machetes, with axes, with knives. You are surrounded by these people. Who knows where that machete or axe is going to end up?

We ran into a demonstration another time and right beside us there were two shots, and a guy beside us just dropped dead. We couldn't find the killer. Was the right person shot, or was it meant for us? You don't know. The only thing you know is somebody beside you just got shot.

# Afghanistan, 2006-07

The two artillery troops were right near each other. This is pretty early in the tour. A white unmarked vehicle starts driving towards the other troop. Just think, a white unmarked vehicle, driving towards machine guns, two howitzers, military vehicles, everything pointed outwards. These idiots were driving towards all this and they weren't stopping.

The other troop fires off a couple warning shots to say, wake up—you're in Afghanistan, driving towards army guys! So they stop, get out, pull out their AKs and start firing back. And we had 50-calibre machine guns. So they Swiss cheesed the truck and one of the guys.

It turned out to be the governor's brother. He was ANP (Afghanistan National Police), they were trying to get to the compound that was on the other side of us, and they thought they could just drive through. It would have been okay if they hadn't gotten out and started firing. I don't understand what they were thinking, but it happened pretty fast.

As soon as it happened, all of our guys went out to do first aid, tried to stop the bleeding. The medic went out there and was working. I think we saved one, but the other, we lost him. It was a mess. We had to move out of there. We were too close to the town so we had to go back out to the desert, to another position in the middle of nowhere, where nobody would come up.

# Former Yugoslavia, 1992

When we first got to Yugoslavia to do the mine awareness training, we had no idea what munitions were in use. We set about trying to find out what munitions were over there, because there were a lot of them. There were over seven million mines buried in the Croatian border area alone.

Our Operations Manager managed to get hold of this Serb colonel, who was in Belgrade at the time. Our team, there were three of us plus a translator, were to travel to Belgrade, which meant that we had to go across the demilitarized zone, which was about a kilometre wide. This was at a place called Osijek. The war was still raging in this area, and the town of Osijek was being shelled by 155-mm and 120-mm mortar and artillery shells.

At the border roadblocks, the people occupying them were usually drunk by ten o'clock in the morning, and it didn't get better as the day progressed. Initially they might offer to have a drink with you, but after a while they just got belligerent and nasty. We had our translator with us, a young lady, I would guess mid-twenties, very attractive. She was actually of Hungarian descent, but she had married a Serb, so her last name was of Serb origin.

This one female Croatian soldier came over and demanded to see her papers. When she showed them to her, she recognized the Serbian name so she called her—gang, I call them, they were thugs with weapons—and they started to make a big deal about this girl and her Serb name. Of course, they had this hatred of Serbs in Croatia and they wanted to take her away. We actually had to produce our weapons and fend them off. Finally, they said, "Okay, you can take her across, but don't bring her back."

So we got into Belgrade, and we got to this colonel who was going to give us the lowdown on all the types of munitions they were using. The first day went by and he never showed. Second day, never showed. Third day, more excuses, more excuses, so finally we said, obviously we aren't going to get to see this guy, so we made arrangements to come back.

Going back through another crossing, they told us we would have to have a 30-minute wait, we were delayed on the crossing. So we sat down, and a couple of soldiers there said, "Would you like a beer?" One of the things over there is, if you don't drink with them, then you're not a man. It's a macho thing. So we sat down with them and had a beer, and we got talking. You don't talk about the war. We got talking about Canada, and this, that, and the other. These people we were having the beer with were a mortar platoon. They have all these 120-mm mortars lined up in the field for as far as you can see.

Finally they said we could go. They de-mined the road for us—they had the mines on large boards so they can pull them across the road and block the road, so they can pull them away quickly and make the road open. The barriers were lifted, and we went across.

We'd no sooner got to the other side of the crossing when they shelled us. They fired their 120-mm mortars at us and in our vicinity for approximately 20 minutes. I tell you, if I could have gotten back across there, I would have throttled them—geez, I was mad. When the first round hit, the concussion was tremendous. I'm quite a big man, and the concussion hit me and I felt all the muscles in my body suddenly relax. The young lady who was with us, the translator, lost control of her bowels. She made quite a mess.

We got into the basement of a building, and she was just beside herself, and at that instant she quit work. She refused to work with us any further because what we did was just a bit too dangerous for her, and she didn't like it. Once we got a lull in the shelling, we jumped back in our vehicle and took off, helter-skelter, back through the town.

## Golan Heights, 1999

The greatest threat over there was the minefields that are all still in place. Some of them are fairly well marked; they're certainly marked on the Israeli side fairly well, but they are not well marked on the Syrian side. They used to be, but if they're marked with any sort of proper fencing, those are attractive items when the farmers were dirt poor—what's the best way to keep my sheep in its pen? Steal this fence over here. So it was more by accident that minefields would be uncovered.

There was an incident where a couple of Austrians that were killed, not a year and a half before I got into the theatre. They had come across smugglers from Syria coming into the Golan Heights over the mountains, the mountain passes there. These guys were nothing more really than criminals, smuggling black market stuff back and forth between the Golan and Syria. The Austrians were shot up because they saw something that they shouldn't have seen. It had nothing to do with Syrian or Israeli military, they were in the wrong place at the wrong time.

## Haiti, 1995-96

The situation was always very hostile. The gangs would take control of a portion of the city. Anyone who walks into that portion of the city will pay with their life. You couldn't go and establish yourself in that portion of the city without these people knowing. So they were controlling pieces of the city. Cité Soleil was one of the worst places to go. We used to go over there all the time because we were UN, we were okay, but anybody else couldn't walk in that territory. They would have gotten killed.

Death is routine, a normal part of life here. We had to deal with that. We had to deal with all those dead bodies. We tried not to touch them but we had to sometimes look at them, who are they, are they one of ours? That was the scary part. In the time that I was there, six months, and from what I heard from the people that took over from us, we only lost one, which is a pretty good record.

## Bosnia, 1994

One time we actually had to insert ourselves in a Croatian compound overnight to see where they were hiding their weapons. We went three times, and we didn't find anything, so we were starting to get a little annoyed. They were saying that we were picking on them, but we weren't because we knew they had weapons, we just didn't know exactly where.

As a team of three guys, we just kind of inserted ourselves in there, and observed them, and we could right away tell where the weapons were. The rest of our guys were at the camp, waiting for a call from us, and we got them in and removed the weapons. It wasn't on the books; I look at it now and think, wow, it was cool to do, but stupid also. A million things could have gone wrong. But you don't realize that at the time, you just focus on accomplishing your mission.

## Afghanistan, 2006-07

When we first got there, the threat was ambush. It wasn't suicide bombers like it is now. We moved during the day because they ambushed at night. When you think about it, that's ridiculous because when you move through Kandahar, it's a city, it's just madness, the cars, and the people. There's no way you could get by anyone. But we'd drive through that with the guns.

Near the end we switched. We never drove during the day because of suicide bombers. The ambush threat went way down. But the troops before us, the ones we replaced, they were ambushed. They were really pissed off about being ambushed. They had all their armour replaced before we got there. You could still see the bullet holes all along the side of the vehicles, and shrapnel embedded in the charge bag canisters.

At night you could sit there in the desert and you could see ambushes light up the convoys. When the convoy drivers started off the tour they were all young and happy and bright. By the end of the tour they were old men. They had totally aged. It was bizarre.

I don't think the Taliban understood the guns; I don't think they understood what a rich target that was, or how much damage it would have done if they would have hit them. I think they thought we could just swing the guns backwards. But we got really lucky; it never happened. Our convoy would go in and the next convoy would be hit.

## Former Yugoslavia, 1992

Zagreb airport, in Croatia, is quite a large airport—it's the main airport for their country. The Serbs had evacuated and driven out; the French were supposed to be moving into there, and prior to that, they had to clear it of explosives. I was tasked to supervise the French so they would know what they were looking for, what kind of munitions and booby-traps they could expect.

I was in Daruvar at the time, which is about a three-hour drive from Zagreb. At about three o'clock in the morning, the phone went off in our operations room. It was my warrant officer, who was with this Serb engineer captain. I had got a bit of a bonding thing going when I was getting information from him; we'd sort of become buddies. I'd made contact with him several times, gone to his unit so we could find out what munitions were what and how they functioned.

He was very concerned, because he had helped set up the booby traps and the explosives in the Zagreb airport. My warrant officer told him that I was going in there to help the engineers take it all apart, and this captain became quite emotional, and said "No, he'll be killed."

He started to tell him all of the munitions that were there, where they were, how they were set up, and this warrant officer phoned at about three o'clock in the morning to relay all this to me. He literally saved my life. If I'd gone in there not knowing what he told me, I would be dead today. There were some booby traps that we were not aware of, and they were very, very sophisticated. They were factory-made, and each one had five different ways of going off. We had no idea that they had that kind of technology.

These were placed hither and thither in the airport, on the runways, in the buildings, throughout the entire infrastructure. Even their toilets—they have these little foot holes, and you squat and do your business through a hole in the ground—they placed pressure-activated mines in the bottom of these places, so eventually enough weight would be on top of the mine and it would be activated. And under the airport itself there were tunnels that were packed full of explosives. We pulled in excess of 14 tons of explosives out from underneath the runway. And every so often there would be a booby trap tucked in with the explosives.

I would have gone in without knowing about any of this, and feeling quite safe, too, quite positive that I could do the job and not get hurt. However, once that phone call came in, I realized I would have been out of my depth, and probably killed. So I left a couple of hours early and got down there, and I was able to brief everybody before they got started, and that probably saved a lot of lives too.

# 7

# SUPPLY

From underwear to armoured vehicles, the Canadian Forces have to provide every conceivable item its soldiers could require while on mission. However, all soldiers know that the equipment doesn't always perform the way it's intended. A good deal of creativity is sometimes needed to get things working right. But from the food they eat to the weapons they carry, our soldiers have strong opinions on the supplies they are given.

## Qatar, 1990

We were issued what was called a Tilley hat. These came from Toronto. The Canadian Forces bought these Tilley hats and they were extremely good because they shaded you from the sun, which was extreme. The RCR thought the Tilley hats were too white, so they took all the Tilley hats and dunked them into these big vats of very strong tea to give them a darker, more sandy colour, which worked very well. One of the advertising things they said about the Tilley hat was that it was so durable that you could pass it through one end of an elephant, get it out the other, dust it off and put it back on your head and it would still work fine. I didn't try that myself.

## Afghanistan, 2006-07

In our first month in the desert, we were down to just rations and water at one point because it took a while for all the aid packages and stuff from home to start coming. So you're stuck eating IMPs (Individual Meal Packs). Literally, to cook your IMP, you throw it on a rock and 15 minutes later it's hot enough to eat. Some of my guys, there were only certain meals they'd eat. They wouldn't eat the main meals. Once it started rolling, our quartermaster got so many dollars a day, and a lot of that money they spent on junk food.

## Qatar, 1990

Defence research had been doing some trials on these sniffers, designed to be set up about a mile out from your camp. These sniffers would tell you if a biological or chemical agent was being dispersed in your area, and you'd get an advance warning. They hadn't actually been used very much, and now they had the chance to use it in the field, so we said yes, by all means, we'd love to have it there. The only sniffer devices we had were for very close range, whereas these would give us advance notice of maybe 15 to 20 minutes.

So these devices were set out, one at each corner about a mile out from the base, and they were hooked into the system. Unfortunately, they kept giving us false readings—at least we think they were false readings. Nobody ever got sick despite the readings, anyway. Eventually we stopped paying attention to it— we were in and out of the chemical and biological suits all the time because this thing kept giving off alarms. I'm not sure what it was sniffing, I don't know what kind of vapours were coming out across the desert all the time, but it was detecting something, which proved not to be of any harm to us.

We were always climbing into what we called the "poopy suit", the chemical/biological suit. It doesn't breathe very well; you wouldn't want air passing through it because you would get contaminated with the biological agents. Once you put one of those on you were in an instant sauna. I've been in that mask so many times, for so many hours, I got quite tired of seeing the inside of them, especially in the Gulf War in 40 degree weather in the evening. You can just imagine what it's like during the daytime.

# Afghanistan, 2003

The food initially sucked because it was a contracted kitchen for the theatre activation team. I don't know how those guys survived for so long on that stuff. Some of the time you had food shortages, so we were mandated a day of IMPs every few days, but once the actual food services contractors got set up in the main part of Camp Julian the food was outstanding. We didn't want for anything from a food point of view. A national pizza chain across Canada brought in all the ingredients for pizzas on

Remembrance Day, and that was a big morale boost. They sent all the ingredients over and then the cooks cooked them in the camp facilities.

# Afghanistan, 2006-07

The Canadian kit is very good. I can't complain about anything we had. Everyone likes their own kind of thing, but I think our kit is way better. Some vehicles not so much. The kit is way better than it used to be.

Our RSM (Regimental Sergeant-Major) got us what I called a gift bag. You'd go to the QM (Quarter Master) and sign for this paper bag and it would have a headlamp, and all of this little stuff we used to always have to buy.

If you went through the chain of command and said I think we should have this, and it was justified, they would go out and buy it. They got us headlamps, they got us Israeli bandages, and new tourniquets that are outstanding, miles ahead of the old field dressings we used to carry. Everyone's got night vision, everyone's got thermal devices on their vehicles. When I was there we had one vehicle with thermal devices, now all the vehicles have it. Some have electronic warfare devices now.

Every rotation it just gets better and better. Like the artillery: we started off with regular guns, now they have all the digital systems on them. You don't even use the sights any more. You look at a screen, traverse and elevate until a circle shows up. It's all automatic. The guns are more and more accurate. Just a big jump in technology. It's like the artillery stepped out of World War II and stepped into this millennium.

We were the first country to use the M777 (155-mm artillery pieces) in combat. They're outstanding. They aren't high-maintenance, but you have to keep them clean. The guys really love working on the guns. There were some issues, I had some hydraulic issues, but never any big problems.

## Cambodia, 1993-94

A lot of MREs (Meals Ready-to-Eat), we moved a lot of MREs. I don't know exactly what they were doing with them, because they were the most foul-tasting things in the world, these crappy American MREs. If you ate them too long, you started crapping white because they were packed with paraffin wax.

The food was Canadian mess food, it was good. I have always maintained that the Canadian military has the best cooks in the world. I'll tell you, though, the seventh week in a row that I had pizza on a Thursday, it got a little thick. They tried the whole line, the more they made it like at home the worse it got, so every once in a while we got our steak and fried eggs, and for New Year's they brought in this huge side of beef and did prime rib. But you know, that just made it worse. That just made you miss home even more.

# 8

# INTERNATIONALS

Canada does not perform its international commitments alone; much of the work involves soldiers from other NATO and UN peacekeeping countries. Canada's unique position in the world means that relations with other countries are typically good, but our veterans often have their own take on the soldiers from other nations they meet and work with.

In recent years, many more nations have offered their soldiers for UN service, making peacekeeping a truly global effort, but also leading to unique situations with soldiers who don't have Canada's long tradition and experience in international deployment.

# Cambodia, 1993-94

It was the largest UN undertaking in history, the biggest UN tour ever—I think it still is, actually. There were a lot of first-time countries there, like Japan. Hungary sent a battalion of convicts. The Polish sent their troops unarmed, which just made for jokes.

The main two helicopter providers were the Russian military and Canadian Helicopters Inc., and those civilians were crazier than everybody else combined. I mean, I was only a kid, and a lot of these guys wouldn't take me seriously because they were, like, my age now. A lot of them were retired military.

One guy I met had been to El Salvador, he'd done all this crazy stuff. He also did firefighting in northern Alberta and Saskatchewan in the off-season. So this guy never stopped flying, never saw his family. He was constantly getting crap, as a civilian pilot. He got crap one time for coming in with palm leaves on his skids because he'd been flying so low. Rumour had it that he had flown into Vietnam accidentally.

Because we were right across the street from the airport, once Canadian Helicopters Inc. showed up they would just hang out at our mess, because it was only, whatever, like a buck a beer. It was common practice for them to buzz us at six in the morning, just BANG-BANG-BANG-BANG-BANG as they went over at 50 feet. There's no FAA there, so what are you going to do, argue with them?

There were a lot of civilians there, employed by the UN. Tons. They were all there getting polling equipment set up, doing the census, explaining—no one among the locals had a clue what it was all about, because a lot of these guys hadn't even been born the last time they held a democratic election. We brought in a local who had been educated in Britain, and he came in to explain to some people how the whole thing worked.

## Golan Heights, 2002

The Japanese troops beside us were great, just the friendliest guys. Their ranking structure is very different. You have your officers' mess, senior NCOs' mess, and junior ranks' mess, and there's not a lot of people, so each mess is very small, the junior ranks mess being the biggest one. So other than their officers, whether they were senior NCOs or not, they all came to the junior ranks mess. They would come in every night with their snacks that were sent to them from home, and they're all different, things that you never would get in Canada. All their different little chips and snacks—squid chips and stuff.

We all really wanted to interact and learn from each other, and try to teach each other some of our languages, so that at least we could communicate. They were always happy. It was just phenomenal. Probably the most respectful people I've ever met as well, as far as UN countries, dealing with them.

The only Poles that we only had to deal with at all were their MPs, who would come over to our side every once in a while because they worked directly with our MPs. Other than that, they stayed to their own side. They were notorious for being not quite above board. They got nailed just before we got there for a huge black market thing. They were dealing outside the camp the locals with cigarettes and stuff. So we were happy to stay separate from them.

## Haiti, 1995-96

We dealt with the Pakistanis. Like with any other country, you had to learn how they work. For example, there were checkpoints in different places in the city. When it was time for prayer, they put their little mat there and they pray, so the checkpoint is nothing to them anymore. The security is gone. However they are very serious soldiers. They were not as flexible as we are. It was either yes or no. They didn't allow the Haitians to get too close to them. Basically the counterintelligence was not done by the Pakistanis, it was done by the Canadians.

They were guarding the airport because that's where the Maple Leaf camp was. The Pakistanis had the airport and they were also working at the UN headquarters. Or we had them with the civilian police, and doing patrols in town at night. So that was the extent of the Pakistanis we had over there. Other than that, going and talking to the public, it was the Canadians that did that.

## Rwanda, 1994-95

The relationship with the other UN soldiers was excellent. We were all in the same boat and it was not the time to start arguing or fighting over a bottle or water or something like that. We all had a job to do and I think we all were doing it to the best of our ability. Of course some people did not have the ability or the training or the education that the Canadians had; we are very fortunate that we have such a professional army, well trained, well educated, well disciplined, and so on. Some of those African countries that were part of our group just do not have that luxury. You have to take somebody with the good and the bad based on his ability.

The Canadians had very good training compared to African soldiers coming from, say, Zimbabwe, or Namibia, or Congo. These officers were very willing to do the job and they were capable and some were excellent, but sometimes they just didn't have the training, the ability to do what we wanted them to do. But the respect that we had amongst ourselves was and is very good.

## Former Yugoslavia, 1992

We had to teach other UN soldiers about mine awareness. Every new group that came in would request our services, and we would be dispatched to them and we would give them the lecture.

Sometimes it was two hours, sometimes it was four hours. The French engineers got the full-blown lesson. If they were just infantry, they got just the two-hour presentation, because it was just designed to teach them "don't touch it", whereas the engineers were taught how to disarm things and make everything safe, so there was a lot more to those lectures.

We would go out to these units, and we could do maybe 20 to 30 people at a time if it was just the presentation, so we would be there maybe a week teaching them about the mines and booby traps that were in the area. With the French, we were down at the Zagreb airport area for two weeks teaching them. That was a bit different because we had to teach it in French, and I'm not Franco. I'm strictly Anglo. The driver I had at the time did all the lectures and I supported him.

We interacted a lot with the other peacekeepers, and then when we got the chance we would break open a bottle and tell stories, exchange experiences. Mostly it was a chance to relieve tension and have a laugh, especially when we were with the British or the Dutch, as their English was excellent.

The Argentineans were very serious soldiers. They didn't speak our language, and we had to go through a translator, so there wasn't that much interrelating with them, but you could tell that they were very appreciative of what we were doing. They also were very frightened by the presentation we gave them because we were giving them the live munitions. Everything we did in these presentations was with live munitions. When they would see us screw the fuse into the live mine they would start packing up.

But they had to see it; they had to know what the real one looked like and how to do it. So we would actually put all the live pieces together and then arm it, to show them that it can be armed safely, and it can be disarmed safely. We did it with the live munitions so that they had the confidence to know that, okay, this is the way it's done and it does work.

## Cambodia, 1994

There were a number of problems with other military down the road from us. There was the Bulgarian contingency and it was the first time the Bulgarians had contributed to a UN theatre. They had basically taken people who were going to go to jail for minor offences and told them, "You can avoid jail if you go into the army and go over to Cambodia and serve a tour." They pretty much staffed their contingent that way.

As these troops are in Cambodia talking to other real soldiers and finding out about such concepts as UN pay, which they weren't getting, they went back and pretty much mutinied. They ended up having to shackle them all up and put them on a plane back to Bulgaria and bring real troops in. And then the next group that came in, there was a shootout at their camp because they got to playing cards with some of the Khmer Rouge mucky-mucks in the area. The card game got out of hand and one side started accusing the other side of cheating and guns and grenades came out.

There was more than one example of that over there. That was one of the earlier times when the UN had put other than mainstream troops on the ground—you know, other than Canadians, Dutch, Swedes, the usual suspects. We had a number of African nations: troops from Ghana had basically showed up, had no uniforms, didn't have anything. UN had to fully kit them out. Tunisians flew over with sandbags, because they didn't know if they could get sand in Cambodia.

## Afghanistan, 2006-07

The Dutch showed up with a Panzer 2000, which was basically the same as our guns but with a giant Panzer body, it's huge, like 20 million dollars. The only problem was that the air conditioning wasn't working in the vehicle, their electronics would shut down at 40 degrees Celsius. Their gun shut down and that was it, it was out of action.

We had some Danish radar guys, we had the Dutch guys,

we played soccer with them, played football with them, and we hung out. We took over from the Dutch in Martello, the second time, and they're really approachable, pretty friendly guys. We're artillery so we worked with the Dutch a little bit because the Dutch are artillery. They had some trouble integrating into our artillery. They weren't as accurate at first; it took them a little while to get on board with us.

I know some of the command post staff, they had some issues at first, but I think any country, same as when we worked with the Americans. It takes a little while to get synced. It took a while for the Americans to trust us because I think they had some issues with the Brits. Things happen, people get a little nervous. But they started to trust us more and more.

I think Americans like to use close air support. They have a lot of that, there's always something up there. My buddy was a FOO (Forward Observation Officer) and they called us the most murderous SOBs in the valley. Another bunch of Americans called us Red Mist, because that's all there was left. They had all that kind of jargon.

# Golan Heights, 1999

We were the contact with the Syrian liaison forces and we had an Israeli liaison officer, which was essentially assigned to the Canadian organization who we dealt with very well. He was a very personable, friendly guy, actually an American who went back to Israel, I think it was at the beginning of the '67 war, moved back there and lived back in Israel. He was very friendly, but even being an American, now back in the Israeli army, he was not open with intelligence. We couldn't question him or get any real information from him.

I was the contact for the other UN soldiers there, being the operations manager. Not so much with the Poles because they were on the other side of the border in Syria. Most of their basic dealings came through the UN camp in Syria. There were two camps, Camp Ziouani on the Israeli side and Camp Faouar on the Syrian side. I had a fair amount of interaction going to meetings at Camp Faouar with the operations staff. The operations staffs from every contingent would get together and have meetings and discussions, but we dealt more with the Poles because they were right beside us. The Poles had only been there a few years, but the Austrians, as far as I know, had been there for a good ten years or so.

We had pretty cordial relations with them all. It's a little more difficult because the language of the UN is English. Some countries' English ability is obviously less than desired for a UN operation. The Austrians were pretty good because most of their officers spoke very good English and I think they must have been instructed in English or something from a NATO perspective.

The Poles weren't members of NATO, and they didn't have a lot of exposure to English-speaking armies. Their soldiers could hardly speak English at all, although that's a requirement to be there. Some of their officers, particularly the key contacts, spoke fairly good English. They had an information officer there who was my contact all the time because he was also their translator, and their second in command of the battalion was pretty good in English as well.

They over-rank a lot of their people, and basically bring them into operations ranked lower. Their information officer was actually a major back in Poland; however, he was a captain in the operation. Their second in command was a major in operations, but he was colonel back in Poland. It's not because their rank levels aren't capable, it's simply because the more senior ranks have better English ability.

Canada was not authorized, based on our ROE (Rules of Engagement) from Ottawa, to use deadly force to protect equipment. We could use deadly force only to protect other UN personnel. The Japanese could only use deadly force to protect Japanese personnel. They couldn't shoot an infiltrator in a camp that threatened a Canadian. So as the operations officer, I couldn't allow Japanese soldiers to man the gates, and Canadians had to do that fully. Canadian soldiers at the corporal, private level don't understand those sorts of national, political issues. All they do is complain, how come we're on gate duty all night long when the Japanese don't have to do it.

In general, there was no tension between the different contingents. It was more convincing soldiers that you have to exercise backbone. Because some of them were veterans of the UN in Bosnia, and because it wasn't a shooting war, they would let their guard down.

# Afghanistan, 2003

Afghanistan is one of those unique environments where NGOs do not want to be associated with a military presence. At that point in time the majority of Afghans believed that the military presence there was not conducive to reconstruction. Afghanistan has had a long and troubled history when it comes to foreign militaries. They haven't welcomed too many foreign armies, nor will they welcome too many foreign armies in the future with much fanfare.

The NGOs know that local Afghans that they work with and deal with, the majority, although they have nothing personally against us, they believe that we are doing a good job too, but they don't want to be too closely linked with us in case things go wrong.

Some of them believe that the closer they operated to us, the more difficult for them to have their own autonomy on projects and things that they wanted to do. Organizations like DART have the same issue. They are not in Sri Lanka or any of those other places from a military point of view, they are strictly humanitarian; it's just that as military, we're more flexible, more deployable and can be given tasks that NGOs can't always do. That means you can't develop those NGO links beforehand, so it's really hard to take them when you need them for a humanitarian operation.

We didn't develop the necessary close working relationships with a lot of NGOs in the Bosnia days, so when we got to Afghanistan it wasn't surprising to me that we didn't have a close operating relationship. We're always trying to build those, and obviously the people in Afghanistan in Kandahar right now have better relations with NGOs than we had to start off with. It's always building.

# 9

# LOCALS

Canadians know that, as foreigners occupying another country—even as UN or NATO representatives—it's important to be on good terms with the local population. Whether handing candy out to children, feeding villages, or just consulting local authorities or elders, Canadian soldiers must be as conscientious in dealing with people they meet as they are of any other part of their work. Our peacekeepers are well known for developing good relations with the local populace, and their diplomacy and tact win them friendship almost everywhere they serve.

# Former Yugoslavia, 1992

There was a young girl, about 17 when I ran into her, in a business school. I was giving a lecture on the dangers around the Daruvar area. She came up to me afterwards and spat at me. I looked at her and said, "What did you do that for?" She spoke very good English, and she told me that she was really ticked off with me because I had cohorted with Serbs in order to get the information that I had. I told all of the students there that the information I had was as a result of good relations with Serb engineer officers. For the most part, they accepted it.

But this girl didn't see it that way at all. I asked her why she hated the Serbs so much, and it turned out her friends had all been raped and murdered in front of her, and she had been sent back to tell the story. At that time, she was 17, and this had happened about a year before. The intense hatred in her face I will never forget. I can see her face right to this day.

The hatred was the biggest thing over there. I can't put it into words—never in all my life have I seen or heard anything that could compare to the hatred that they have for each other.

# Qatar, 1990

When we first went over, we were filled with trepidation. We didn't know what was going to happen. We didn't know if the locals were going to be friendly to us. In fact, there were some reports that some of the locals were attempting to shoot at us with sniper rifles, but they were tracked down by the local bodyguards and were taken away. That's just a rumour. I don't know if anyone validated that, but we were always on guard.

One of our chaps, our transport sergeant, was detailed

to go into Doha from Canada Dry 1 camp and source some four-wheel-drive vehicles that we could rent. He took off in an ordinary car that had been loaned to him. When he got down near the area, he pulled into a walled parking lot, and just as he pulled in, this group of Arabs started attacking his vehicle, banging and beating on the vehicle. He was quite scared, so he put it into reverse and backed out of there and took off back to Canada Dry 1 camp. He told the military police what had happened, and the military police went and got the local police, and he and the military police and the local police went down to this location.

When he pulled in there, the local police started to laugh. He had pulled into an area where locals go if they want a migrant worker. So there were 20 or 30 of these migrant workers waiting for someone to pull in and give them a job, and they all wanted to be first, so that's why they were beating on his car. Of course, the feeling that we had when we first arrived, not knowing what the heck was going on and not knowing some of the customs there, all led to this rather funny story of him being scared.

# Cambodia, 1994

The various factions would set up roadblocks for any reason, not the least of which would be to extort money out of the UN guys. Other countries would come along and either get into firefights with them or get held up for hours and hours and hours. The Canadians learned very early on that all they wanted was a wave and a smoke. Cigarettes were so cheap, three bucks a carton, so myself and the other section commanders and many of the other troopies would go to the market and we'd buy a few cartons of cigarettes and take them on every road move.

It wasn't very long before we'd start to come up to a roadblock and they'd be moving the roadblock before we'd even started slowing down because they saw the Canadian flags on our bumpers. We'd slow down, they'd be waving and smiling. We'd throw out a few packs of cigarettes and they'd just wave us on through.

That's the kind of Canadian ingenuity that you don't see

anywhere else. You don't have to shoot your way through stuff to get what you want. And we learned that there. Canada's always done that differently. The tours that I've been on and the tours that I've seen them putting together, a big part of the training is getting into the culture. This is good manners, this is bad manners. For example, you don't go pat a Cambodian child on the head like you would in Canada. You can get shot for that. You don't sit down with the bottom of your feet pointing at these people—it's offensive. You learn things like that.

We'd try to learn various things in their language before we went over. Not the least of which was 'stop', 'hands up', 'stop or I'll shoot'. We'd learn stuff like this so you wouldn't get yourself into a situation for no other reason than language barrier.

That led to the name that we had given them. It's not very politically correct nowadays, but of course any soldier that you talk to will tell you that no matter where they had been, you would always come up with a name for the locals. In Israel, it was the Heebs. In Egypt it was the Gyppos. In Cambodia, we would call the locals cho-hips. And nobody could figure out how we came up with the name cho-hip. What happened was, when we were getting our language training to be able to communicate with them, everything was unfolding so fast. The first rotation had just gone over and now we're pre-training for the second rotation.

The stuff came directly from the Canadians already in Phnom Penh. They'd write this stuff down from their translators. The translators would say it. They'd write it down phonetically and fax it to us so we could practice it. One of the things we'd gotten the word 'stop' and the way it was written, it looked like you would pronounce it 'cho-hip'. Once we got over there, any time we would challenge these people, it would be 'cho-hip', and they'd look at us like we had two heads.

Finally we went to a translator, and he said, "What are you saying?" And we said, "Well, we're trying to tell them to stop." And he said, "No, no. 'Stop' is 'chohp', not 'cho-hip'." But cho-hip just kinda stuck after that. Any time you talk to someone who was over there and they're telling a story, it'll usually be about 'cho-hips'.

With these people, it wasn't garbage until they threw it

away. The thick plastic wrappers on our MREs, they'd get two of them and wear them as shoes, one on each foot. You'd see them in the old US Army trucks, broken down at the side of the road, transmission lying on the road beside the truck, and they're squatted over this thing with a hammer, a pair of pliers, and a screwdriver. You'd drive past there three or four hours later and that truck is gone. It was unbelievable.

On one of our convoys, we had a full load of paint. I can't even remember what it was being used for, this thick yellow paint, almost like the stuff you'd paint lines in a parking lot with. We were taking it up north to one of the other units, and the roads were so rough, one of the cans busted open, and this yellow paint was dripping off the back of the truck. So we're sitting by the side of the road eating lunch, and they're catching it in cans and pails and anything else. And for what? What are you going to do with it? Do you even know what it is? Doesn't matter—they're going to figure out what it is, and they'll figure out something to do with it.

Probably one of the most heartbreaking moments was, on more than one occasion, a mother would bring a very young child or a newborn to the front gate and try to give the child away, telling us, take the child to Canada and give it a better life. It's kind of tough to swallow.

## Cyprus, 1991

The interesting part of my tour was that the guy whose observation post was directly opposite mine on the Greek side was actually from Toronto. He went to Greece to visit his grandfather and they took him and put him in the army for three years. He was always asking about the Leafs.

You got close enough to talk to either side, because when you changed shift with your partner, you patrolled the area as you went back to your position, and on your way you walked by and talked to them. It was that peaceful at that time, there wasn't anything that was going to brew up. On the political side of the house they were never going to agree, but the buffer zone seemed to work.

# Haiti, 1995-96

Our intelligence sources were all Haitians, normal people. Haitians live not like you and me for the next year, for the future. They live for the next five seconds. They could be dead in five seconds. Their first religion is Catholic, their second religion is voodoo. So you could have at any time a priest, a voodoo priest that says you're dying, and the person believes, so he lets himself die. So voodoo is very strong there. The hoogah, which is the voodoo priest, has a lot of power.

But the people there in Haiti are just normal people living one second at a time because the next second they could be dead. People would buy oranges in the corner street for let's say one or two gourds—we used to get four to five gourds for one dollar. So they'll buy two or three oranges for two gourd, half a dollar or less, and resell them down the street to make a little bit of money to buy a little bit of rice to feed the family. They live one day at a time. Haitians, they're either poor, or they're rich. There is nothing in between.

If you're rich you live off in the mountains where the weather is maybe three or four degrees lower. If you're poor you live in the capital, which the capital was built for six hundred thousand people, and there were three million people in there. They were all stacked, tiny houses the size of my office, and you have a family of five living in there. But they don't stay in the hut. They are on the street, looking for work, looking for food. You can see a Haitian looking through garbage, trying to find a pair of shoes or finding a sandal one colour and a sandal another colour, or trying to find a bag with leftover food to take home for later that night.

When you approach a Haitian they're very careful. Don't forget, we were the only white people in that country. There were other white people, from embassies and that, but for military force the Canadians were the only white people. We learned when we approached them, they didn't smile. They were very cautious. They don't like weapons, and we were carrying weapons too. So when they see you and you finally get close enough to them to talk to them, the first thing they do is raise their hands, showing they don't have any weapons. When you go and shake their hands and then they get comfortable, they understand what you are there for. The Canadians on average we had a very good reputation of helping them and trying to bring the country up.

When we met a source, we had to work in Haitian time. If they tell you at one o'clock, it could be anywhere between eight in the morning to six in the afternoon. We used to be there on time at one o'clock and they wouldn't show up. And if you leave, the next morning you try to contact them, they say, well, I was there. What time did you go? At three o'clock. Well, we told you one o'clock. So Haitian time, it's another thing. It's tomorrow, or the next half hour.

Don't forget that these people were all on foot. They're poor and they're in what they call tap-taps. That's like their taxis, little Toyota trucks. They put 50, 60 people in there and they go from place to place and they drop them and they pay them 50 cents to go to another place. There is no such thing like in Canada where you pay and get in. We used to say that on a tap-tap there is always room for one more.

## Central African Republic, 1998

I didn't think it existed in Africa anymore, but we saw villages where people had never seen a white person before. We were the first white people and they touch your skin and face. In Africa you still have the jungle and you still have the monkeys and you still have the people hunting and there's always food. Nothing to go to the market and see monkeys as food, and they had cows, and snakes, and things like that, and that's normal for them.

## Cambodia, 1993-94

The best thing about Battambang was that it was the only place you could get a decent burger. They had a great little restaurant that made cheeseburgers. And the Australians had a pretty neat little mess there, so we'd usually spend the night drinking with the Australians, then go back to our hotel and spend the next day driving back.

The local people were pretty awesome. For a country that had been treated so horribly, they were a pretty great bunch of people. We interacted with them a lot—you had to. Actually, our taxi driver, I wrote to him for a couple of months after I got home, and one of my co-workers apparently wrote back and forth with him for years. This guy had no idea when his birthday was because the hall of records had been blown up and his parents had been killed. So he had no idea how old he was. And yet the guy never stopped smiling, and when you realized what they'd seen, the horrible way they'd been treated by the Khmer Rouge, it was incredible.

They were a really good bunch of people, really hard-working people, interesting people. When you went to the Killing Fields, I can't remember the exact name of the actual park, they had a memorial for one of the actual mass graves. It had this thing that looked like a Japanese pagoda, at least three stories tall, about three metres by three metres, and it was just packed with human skulls the whole way up. That kind of stuff got to you after a bit, when you actually saw what they did.

When something happened, everybody sat there and looked but nobody would help. We couldn't understand that. We saw little kids get injured pretty bad, and we'd be jumping out of our trucks and helping, and people would just be standing around watching, not offering help. I don't pretend to understand how that side of the culture works. Maybe you just don't have a lot of respect for life when you've seen so much of it taken away.

## Rwanda, 1994-95

I never dealt with civilians. The only civilians that I saw were dead, and sometimes those that were fortunate to have been transported, but most of them were dying at the Red Cross hospital because the Red Cross hospital had so many injured. They would only treat those who had a chance to survive, and treatment was very basic.

I remember seeing a 16 or 17-year-old girl, sitting on the table in the hospital naked, and she had been hit by grenade shrapnel, all over her body. A nurse with little pliers was trying to find each little piece of shrapnel and she's sitting there without any painkillers, and she's covered in blood all over. That happened all the time. You see a little boy, two years old, like that, crying and screaming and you think, my God.

# Former Yugoslavia, 1992

One day we were driving through and this 16-year-old boy waved us down, and said, "Could you help us?" His parents were afraid to go outside. He took us into his backyard and some 255-mm artillery shells had landed in his backyard and not exploded. It was the time of year when they liked to get their garden going, and they had no food, no electricity, no water, so getting a little garden going was literally a lifesaver to them. And they couldn't go outside because of these unexploded bombs.

Me and my partner neutralized them. We took the fuses out and I put the bomb itself right on my shoulder to carry it as I was going by the house. The woman in the house invited us in, and boy, they really looked after us. We had a big sumptuous lunch, and whatever they could afford to give us they put on the table. I think they must have cleaned out their entire larder, just for the two of us.

They couldn't do enough for us; they kept forcing food on us, and we knew they couldn't afford it, but they insisted that we eat it. We drank their beer and what they called sljvovic, a plum brandy. It's absolutely horrible. They think it's good, they kept feeding us that as well. Then the 16-year-old boy decided that he was going to help me carry this bomb, so I lifted it and put it on his shoulders, and he went right to his knees—it is quite a big, heavy artillery piece.

Those that were still in the area were surrounded by unexploded munitions, and it was our job to take care of that, especially if they were on the routes our patrols were utilizing. Our job was to keep those routes clear. If there were any other things on the side, if a bomb or a missile had been fired from an aircraft and had not exploded, these areas were usually marked and we would take care of them.

There was one I remember very clearly. A family was in the process of slaughtering their pigs. It was that time of year. They also had bees, and these bees were on a big trailer. This aircraft came over and thought it was a group of soldiers with a munitions trailer, and he fired four of his missiles at them. No one was hurt, but one of the missiles hadn't gone off and had buried itself into the ground.

They called us up and said they thought it was a chemical munition, but in fact it was the missile itself was spewing a white liquid from out of the ground, out of the hole it had gone into. When we got there we started digging, and we finally found it about four metres deep in the ground. We got a Norwegian front-end loader to come up with us the next morning, we tied a cable around the missile, and we hooked onto it and pulled it up out of the ground and took it away.

The whole time we were doing it, they kept coming up to us with this plum brandy, and they kept feeding us. We were trying to dig, and that took a lot of energy in this sucking muck that we were in, and they kept giving us little plates of food, sliced meats and things like this, and also sljvovic. It's an insult not to drink it; they get quite upset if you don't take their offer.

## Cambodia, 1994

The first rains of the season, they all shoot into the sky. You ask, "What are you shooting for?" and they say, "We have to bring the fish down out of the sky and into the water." They figure the fish are up in the sky, and you have to shoot them to make them fall down into the lake that didn't exist the day before it started raining. There will be a ditch, bone-dry one day. It starts to rain, they shoot into the sky, and the next day they're pulling fish out of that ditch.

Where'd the fish come from? We were freaked the first time we saw that. We thought, who's the idiot here, them or us? But what they were was mud puppies. They'd burrow down as it dried up, and they can live up to six months in wet mud. Then it rains, they crawl back up to the surface, swim around, and get caught in the net of some Cambodian.

## Bosnia, 2001

I would say most of the people there just want to get on with their lives. I'd go to the Serbs, are the Croats giving you a hard time? They'd say no. How are the Muslims doing? Oh, they're fine. They're sick and tired of wars. It's the few political people that stir things up, get everybody riled up. They're the dangerous ones.

Some guys are screwed up because the war really affected them. We had this old fellow who was being harassed by some Croatians. I think he was the only one left in his village, a village of a couple hundred completely wiped out. He's living in just appalling conditions and he's terrified every night because he's telling us, there's these Croatian guys harassing me. So we told him, we'll start patrolling your area at night time. So we drove the Grizzly through his area. The next time we talk to him he says, you know, I heard a tank last night. They're coming to get me. And I said no, that's us, we're just checking on you to make sure you're all right. So people are obviously affected.

One woman was a teacher before the war. I guess during the war she went crazy. Daily, people were coming up to the gate saying, give me this, or I need a stove, or I need food, or whatever. Our policy, you don't give anything out at the gate, it gets distributed throughout the villages. But she'd come up to the gate and say, I want this, and the guys would say no. So up comes her top. Have a look at these! She's about 55 years old. It's funny how different people have been affected.

I've talked to young children, one girl was 7 years old at the time and she said I hate knives. And I said, why do you hate knives? She said because, when the Serb army came in, the guy rounded up the whole village, and he took one guy from the village who he didn't like, and he slit his throat in front of anybody and said, mess with me and this is what's going to happen to you. She said since then, I hate knives.

This one woman, I gave her a pot set and a bed and a stove, and she broke down bawling. I asked her, through an interpreter of course, what's wrong? She said, "I'm sorry, I feel like a beggar. Before the war I had everything, and now I have nothing." I said, "You're not a beggar, you're a victim. And I'm sorry that I can't do more." I mean, her whole family was living in a woodshed because the house was basically demolished. It was weird, one minute you're getting spit on, and the next minute you're a saviour. That kind of twists you up as well.

I think the most difficult thing that I still deal with today is that every day I was there, every single day, I had to say no to somebody. It's farming season and they need wheelbarrows, so I talk to my boss. Are there any wheelbarrows, or can we get any? No, we don't have any. So you say no to these poor farmers. You go there thinking you can make a difference, and you do make a difference, but it's frustrating, because you can't save everybody. There's always somebody you have to say no to, and that's really frustrating.

## Afghanistan, 2006-07

When we were leaving, for whatever reason, they had hired an Afghan security company to come to our position. They're basically militia guys, in black with AK-47s. These guys came in the gate, and of course they're all cleared for security, and they start wandering around. Imagine, you have your base and suddenly all these Afghan dudes are all over the place checking everything out because they're moving in and they're trying to find the best spots.

We're desperately trying to tear down as fast as possible so we can marshal the trucks and go, and we can only carry so much. Whatever we couldn't carry we disposed of. So we'd put something on the fire to burn and the Afghans would run and grab it. We had a lot of junk food by that time, and we loaded the trucks only as much as we could. The Afghan guys would come in, and they'd be running away with cases of pop and boxes of junk food.

We had a lot of hygiene stuff, so we gave it to them. It's not that they didn't understand toothpaste, but they can't read it or whatever, so they were trying to eat the toothpaste. One of my guys tried to show them how to use e-mail, that got a little out of hand—there's like 30 of them all around him, I had to post a couple guys to make sure nothing happened. My big Lebanese driver, from Montreal, he was Arabic so they could sort of understand him. He was my guy to try and communicate with them to get away from the mortars. It's time to pack up, and literally it was getting dark, these guys were all over the place. It was dicey. It was like leaving Saigon.

## Cambodia, 1993-94

I worked with one female soldier, an infantrywoman from a Toronto Scottish regiment. We had a lot of females on our trip because the service battalion was running the show. But as an infantrywoman, she was a real rarity—and she was very popular. The locals were really weird, though, when they saw her, because she was about their height, but she was relatively well-endowed, and that was just something those women don't see.

Cambodians don't have any concept of your personal space, and here comes me, five nine and 200 pounds and a 48 inch chest, and their men don't have chests. They'd come up and they'd poke me in the chest, to see what's going on, and they'd touch my nose, because their men don't have noses that size. They'd just walk up, and that would be their thing, especially the older women.

## Golan Heights, 1999

I had a fair amount of interactions with locals. I dealt with people on the street, shopkeepers. A lot of the soldiers' interactions within the Golan Heights were in souvenir dealings, and you would always get the pulse of them from stuff like that. Obviously our Ops staff did a lot further work. Some of our Ops staff visited villages in the Golan Heights, just to get an idea.

We would sit at a local café, have a coffee and talk to as many people as we could to find out what the situation was, and to tell you the truth, there wasn't an awful lot of tension at that point in time because the Golan Heights is for the most part abandoned. The Israeli settlers aren't allowed to move into the Golan without strict control by the Israeli government, so you don't have to worry in a village up near the Syrian border that a family of a couple of Israelis will move in there, all of a sudden creating havoc. That kind of stuff doesn't happen.

Every Canadian soldier had a sort of business card with the Canadian flag on it, and many Canadian soldiers have served there in the last 25 years or so. The shopkeepers collected these cards and put them on top of their glass display cases. They tried to say, look, I've got 12 little cards from Canadians here, whereas if you talk to George down the street, he's only got three or four, obviously more Canadians like it here. Very competitive that way.

We tend to be more affluent, and had more money in terms of allowances than either the Poles or the Austrians, so we tended to spend more money in the shops. I wouldn't say we got preferential treatment, but even if the Austrians and Poles were just as polite and friendly, the Canadians were much more attractive as customers because we brought more money with us.

# Cambodia, 1994

I've got a picture of a six-legged cow that used to eat at the side of the road. We used to drive out to this one place to re-supply one of the other NATO countries. This six-legged cow was always in the middle of the town grazing. Quite an oddity. They wouldn't think of euthanizing like we would. Either it'll live or it'll die.

And that's how they treated their people. If kids are born handicapped, in most cases, they'll just take them off into the bush and leave them. I've got pictures of one girl, no one could figure out how she ever survived. We figured she might have had spina bifida or something like that. She walked on all fours because a section of her spine was missing so she couldn't stand up straight. She had full mobility, she just couldn't stand up straight.

There was this one road we used to go down we called Beggar's Alley. All the beggars would line up there because the UN trucks would go through quite frequently. They'd take their little shovels and sticks and whatever and they'd fill in potholes, so as you went by, hopefully, they could get some money from you. But after you went by, if you looked in your rear-view mirror, they would take the dirt back out of the hole, waiting for the next group of trucks to come.

# Afghanistan, 2003

In general the Afghanis were very hospitable. They were guarded about certain things. For the most part the Northern Alliance didn't want to continue active operations. However, they knew that power base and therefore money comes from maintaining your local militia. It's sometimes difficult and I know that it certainly caused a lot of angst in the government to be including what some people considered thugs and warlords in the new government, but they still wield an enormous amount of popular support.

General Hazi Shah Alam was the guy in our area. He had fought the Russians in the Mujahideen, so he held an enormous amount of public support locally. We needed to get those kind of people on our side because it was through him that the local villagers would get an understanding that if General Shah Alam recognizes these people as friends and that we're trying to help the Afghans, then we will accept them into our villages and so on.

He was instrumental in bringing a large group of elders into meetings where we could talk to them from a civic point of view, and say what are the most important projects, what area should we start off with, and sort of bring them into the fold and get them to cooperate more with us. The more we were able to build up a relationship with local villagers, the more those elders would report back to General Shah Alam that, yeah, there's a few visitors into our village and we don't know where they come from, that is, they're Taliban or Al-Qaeda trying to infiltrate back in. Then we were able to plan operations to deal with those kinds of things.

Getting those elders on side and convincing them that they're better off supporting the Coalition forces than the Taliban is difficult because, although those elders are not highly educated, they are very attuned to the political winds. It would be naïve for Canadians to believe that an elder in a village outside of Kandahar does not know what the Canadian public support for the Afghan mission is.

They now very well that they can't necessarily permanently hitch their horse to the ISAF or the NATO cart because they don't know if in two years' time NATO will be there. They may not believe, based on what people in Canada are saying, that Canada will be there in a couple years' time. If the Taliban or Al Qaeda gains control, even regionally, their life may end when ISAF leaves. So they're careful not to commit.

That's not to say they're pro-Taliban and would give information on Canadian movements to insurgents. It just means that they just have to very guarded about how much support they show for a particular force because they've seen it in the past. Foreign armies are like a wind in Afghanistan. They blow in and then they will blow out again, and no one can predict when.

## Sri Lanka, 2005

Word quickly got around, don't be afraid of these people in uniform that are wearing this funny little patch on their shoulders, they're there to help. So much so that they took us into their confidence a lot of times. There's something about going through a village and meeting and talking to the people who have lost family members and having this guy take you into what used to be his house and show you where his children used to sleep and where his wife used to sleep, and he doesn't know where they are. They're gone. The last time he saw them, they were being taken out to sea.

The people that are affected in a disaster like that don't want to see a bureaucrat with a briefcase full of money. For one thing, in a third-world country a lot of that money is not going to filter down to them. Let's face it, there's an element of corruption in a certain number of third-world countries where the DART would deploy to. I'm not saying that takes place in Sri Lanka, but there are a number of countries where that money would not get to the places that need it. It is much more important to see somebody actually out there doing something with the Canadian flag on their shoulder, to see that people are actually directly helping them to get over this.

The tricky thing about the DART is not developing dependency. You don't go in there to deliver something that they couldn't get before the tsunami. It's a little difficult to do that when you have such a medical capability from a western country. Initially we were dealing with the immediate effects of the tsunami and then the tertiary effects from a disease point of view.

But it got the point where there were elderly Sri Lankans that were coming up to the medical clinic wanting Viagra. Obviously outside the scope of the immediate disaster. We tried to assist them, we'd say we don't have that capability, but there are some organizations that come in later on that will be able to help you with those basic medical necessities.

## Cambodia, 1994

When you go to the market, there are all of these kids that want to carry your purchases for you. They walk around with big coolers that are bigger than they are full of ice-cold Coke and stuff to look after you, you know. Nobody has shoes, walking around in the all the garbage and filth. And you give them a buck or two at the end of your shopping trip.

There was this one kid that always seemed to be around when I was there and carried all my stuff for me, so I bought him a pair of flip-flops. First time he's ever owned a pair of shoes in his life! Next day, I'm at the market and he doesn't have his flip-flops and I'm a little worried because knowing this place, the big kids probably held him down and took them. He said, "No, my mother took them away. She says I gotta keep them for good for school."

Can you imagine? I mean, here our kids are screaming before they go to school, they gotta have this label or that label. This kid's mother put flip-flops away so he'd have a good pair of shoes for school. And it just frustrates me to an unhealthy level to see that go on here, how materialistic we've become.

# 10

# BELLIGERENTS

Peacekeepers have the unenviable task of standing between two warring factions to prevent conflicts from restarting, usually without the option of using force. Both factions often see the peacekeeper not as a partner in building a better future, but as an obstacle to their aims—or as an enemy to be defeated. And Canadian soldiers must act in strict accordance with the needs and constraints of their mission when they confront belligerents, whether they are friendly, neutral, or openly hostile.

# Former Yugoslavia, 1992

I call it "peacekeeper in the middle." You're in a situation where you're standing in between the two belligerents, and they're firing over and around you, and every once in a while they take shots at you. That wasn't uncommon. Several of our vehicles had bullet holes in them because some smartass decided to take a pot shot at a UN vehicle. It became quite well known that the Serbs, at least, were not interested in the safety of peacekeepers.

There was one time I was going up into this mountainous village on one of the patrol routes for our infantry. There was a mortar round that had landed, gone into the ground, and had not gone off. Our job was to go up and retrieve it and dispose of it, and make the route safe again for the patrol. I had just stopped our vehicle at the local police station to ask them where this mortar round was located. I went around to the back of the vehicle, when all of a sudden this machine gun went off right behind me, couldn't have been more than 20 paces behind me.

I turned and saw this police officer standing on the steps of his police station. He had just loaded his weapon and was discharging it for the heck of it, knowing full well that I was standing right in front of him and it was probably going to scare the bejeezus out of me. But he got quite a shock because I turned and ran at him. Oh, man, I was pissed off. I just charged right at him and he turned and ran right into the police station and disappeared.

The police chief suddenly stepped out and he says "Are we in trouble?" And I said to him, "No, but you've got an idiot working here." I let him have it, told him what I thought of it. Anyway, the police chief apologized and pointed out where the munition was and we carried it away safely and got rid of it. There were a lot of incidents like that.

# Bosnia, 2001

We actually did a raid on a guy, he owned a couple of factories in the community, and he was suspected of stealing aid, hoarding it, and selling it. Raiding the factory was kind of covert. We deployed outside the town like we were going off doing regular exercises or whatever, and then we went up into the mountains and just shut down all the vehicles for a couple of hours. And then we drove down the mountain, black out drive, and kind of snuck in as best we could.

We went in with all our guys and Grizzlies as well. We did a cordon search, basically our troop surrounded the building with the Grizzlies, and then the other troop went in and they did the actual search inside the building. There were no personnel inside the building, there were no booby traps or anything, so that was fortunate. But we found a load of stolen aid. That was kind of fun. We had to hold onto it as evidence of course until they prosecuted him.

# Former Yugoslavia, 1992

I was down in Sarajevo, and at that time the airport was under siege. Winter was coming on, people were going to be freezing, because everything in the area was being blown to bits, so most of them were living outdoors. So an Italian aircraft took off with fourteen tons of blankets on board, and it was going to fly in and land at Sarajevo. On the way, somebody decided to fire a ground-to-air missile at it, and blew it up in air. It took out the wing and they came down in a fiery ball and landed on a mountain in the area of the Sarajevo airport. The four crew were killed instantly.

The next day, because I have booby trap expertise and all that, I was asked to go with the team to recover the remains. We drove up into the mountains and arrived that night, and we could still see the glow of the aircraft where it had crashed, it was still on fire up on the mountain. We camped that night, and it snowed, too, their first snowfall up in that area, so it was quite cold, but it helped to put out the fire.

The next morning we got up there and realized that animals had got at the remains. We set out these little red flags in the ground wherever we found bits and pieces of the bodies. It looked like a sea of poppies, so many little pieces all over the place. The animals had carted off many of the large pieces.

When we finally managed to combine the pieces and get them into body bags, we had maybe about 25 pounds in weight. That's about all there was left of each human being. So that was very sad. These guys were just flying blankets into the airport to try to help the local civilians.

We put the remains into the ambulance that we had with us. On our way back, we got stopped at a roadblock, where this chap—he looked identical to Sylvester Stallone in the Rambo movies, only much bigger, about six foot six. Bare-chested, bandoliers across his chest, jet black hair, steely, piercing blue eyes. I was quite surprised that this guy was totally sober.

He was in charge of this checkpoint, on this very narrow road. We were coming around a corner and all of a sudden there they were. They pulled these boards with mines on them across in front and behind us, so we couldn't go back or forward. These guys were all well-armed, and there were about 16 of them altogether, all drunk except for Rambo. They were very belligerent, most nasty. They kept us there for over three hours, poking us with their guns. They never took our weapons away, but they kept prodding us, hoping to provoke something.

The only guy there who spoke English was the Rambo chap, and I actually quite admired him because he kept his soldiers at bay, he kept them away from us as much as he possibly could. Then, what appeared to be his girlfriend or his wife showed up. She ended up sitting next to what was their protection, a small machine gun.

These guys were getting more and more belligerent, and getting drunker and drunker, and it looked like it was going to come to a firefight. So the major told me, you man the .50 cal, and you make sure you take out the machine gun first, and then swing it down the line.

Most of them were sitting on lawn chairs down the side of the road, they had a sort of canopy pulled up over top of them to keep the sun and rain off. It would have been quite easy to take them all out. What bothered me was that this guy's wife was sitting there, and she was right in the line of fire. I had to take out the machine gun first, and she was sitting right beside it, so she probably would have been killed as well.

So anyway, they refused to let us go, they insisted on searching our vehicles, and we refused to let them do that. We were guarding these four bodies, and it was paramount to us to get the remains safely back. About three and a half hours later, we decided we were going to fight our way out of there.

We were in contact with Sarajevo, and Sarajevo said no, do not open your vehicles, and do not allow them to search your vehicles. They don't have any right to do that. But within minutes of me having to pull the trigger, it came over the radio, okay, let them look in the back of the vehicles, if that's what they want. And they came over, looked in the back of the vehicle, and opened up one of our lunch boxes, this cardboard box with a few sandwiches in it, and that's all they did. They told us we could now leave, after all that.

And I came so close. I had a round up the spout, a belt of ammunition fed in, and I was ready to pull the trigger. So I was very glad. And when we went round the corner, my heart went right down into my boots. There was a tank sitting there. So we would not have got out of there alive. I still have nightmares over that one.

# Rwanda, 1994-95

It was roadblocks all the time. You didn't have very far to go before you got to a roadblock. In the territory held by the government forces, the roadblocks were manned by the government forces and the soldiers and, very often, by what we called the militia, the Interhamwe. They were the people responsible for most of the massacres. There was no real big problem, sometimes they would see the UN vehicle coming, you'd stop, you would say in French comment ça va, ça va bien, blah blah blah. Then they would look in the vehicle, you would say I am with five journalists, they'd wave you through and that's it. Once you get into the rebel territory it was the same thing. They were sometimes a bit more stiff, more cocky or more on the ball. But you managed to go through.

# Former Yugoslavia, 1992

This happened to us quite a few times. We would get stopped and they'd ask us what's in our vehicle. I'm a pretty big guy, so I had to become quite aggressive sometimes. We were always being accused of carrying weapons and munitions to whoever the opposition was—the Serbs said we were carrying them to the Croatians, the Croatians said we were carrying them to the Serbs. Of course, none of this was true. The stuff I had in my vehicle was just stuff for display in our lectures.

This one captain in particular insisted on looking in the back of our vehicle. I couldn't let him look in there because we had their munitions in it, which we had stolen from them. So here I am with live ammunition and training aids for our lectures, and this guy wants to look in our vehicle. I knew that if he saw what we had in there, he would blow his gasket.

So this guy came up and he started to open up the tarp, pulling the straps off. I told my driver to stay in the front. I went around the back and I undid my flak jacket and made sure he could see that I had my 9 mm pistol inside, and he wouldn't stop. I took his hand away and started doing the straps back up, and he still continued to try undoing the straps, so finally, I slapped him across the yap. Probably the stupidest thing I ever did.

I heard all the weapons behind me, this guy's crew all cocked their weapons when I hit their officer. And the only thing he said to me was "Is your vehicle gas or diesel?" I stepped back and I looked, and said, "It's diesel." "Oh, okay, okay, you can go." Boy, I tell you, I jumped into that vehicle so quick—I thought I had just got us killed, I really did. There were a few incidents like that, where they wanted to search our vehicles, and we just bullied them, basically, into letting us go through their roadblocks. It was about returning their posturing and making yourself look bigger than they did.

The thing with them was you'd look them in the eye the whole time. That was part of their mentality. If you looked them in the eye, you were coming at them straight. And if you said to them, look, get out of my way or I'm going to pull out my weapon and shoot you in the head, and you looked them in the eye the whole time you were saying this and your body position was such that it looked like you were going to do it, they backed down every time. I'm just glad I never actually had to pull my gun.

## Cambodia, 1993-94

We were in Battambang, myself, two other reservists, and my buddy, who was in the RCR. So we were walking to the hotel we were supposed to be in. There only so many hotels—we were only allowed to stay at authorized hotels, and Battambang wasn't really known for its nightlife.

As we were coming into the hotel, four gentlemen—you know what, I don't even know, it could have been six, or maybe it was less, but it seemed a lot bigger at the time—these guys came in wearing non-CPAF uniforms, carrying an array of different equipment, in black uniforms.

There's no doubt in my mind we were dealing with the Khmer Rouge. They were carrying very old M-16s. In what other country are you going to come up a hotel walkway and see guys with RPGs (Rocket-Propelled Grenades) over their soldiers and M-16s, wearing Khmer Rouge uniforms? And there was no movie style—nobody was wearing the scarves around the neck, these guys were the thousand-mile-stare, hard, hard, hard soldiers. Scary hard soldiers.

So we were standing there, and this one reservist, she went up and just started jawing with them. They didn't understand a word she was saying, I guess, but there was a lot of laughing and giggling. Our packet commander just looked at me and the other guys and said, "We are not staying here." So we took the vehicles to a safe compound and parked them, and my buddy and I ended up spending the whole night standing and talking. I mean, we were driving around armed, we had 30 rounds live in our rifles, ready to go, but that's all we carried.

I don't know how concerned the other guys were, but sleeping in the truck in 80% humidity, in 60 degrees Celsius, isn't the easiest thing to do at the best of times. I was totally freaked out by the whole situation. We had been in areas where we could watch firefights, but from a distance. You could hear machine guns going off, you could see tracer, stuff like that. But that's the closest I've been. It was very uncomfortable—there was just a lot of tension there. And there's no doubt in my mind that they were on their way to do something nasty. It's pretty weak, I realize, but that's about how dangerous it got.

## Golan Heights, 1999

There was a Syrian farmer that stepped on a land mine and fortunately he was in the zone where the closest medical facility was the UN medical facility. That was the one time when the Israelis and the Syrians could cooperate. They needed to bring the Syrian over to the Israeli side of the Golan Heights to get him treated and the UN medical facility. Otherwise he wasn't going to make it to Damascus.

The Israelis and the Syrians essentially got together and agreed, okay, open the gates, bring this person in, and the UN was able to evacuate him immediately. If they treated everything with that kind of cooperation there would be a lot less problems. He was actually treated at the Canadian medical facility and transferred to the UN medical facility.

# 11

# DOWNTIME

There is little time for relaxation on most UN and NATO missions, so soldiers try to make the most of their break from their mission. Although t hat time off can have both advantages and drawbacks, there is no question that it is well-deserved.

# Former Yugoslavia, 1992

My son was so jealous—here I was, 40 years old and going to a Guns N' Roses concert. We had a 72 hour pass, and Hungary wasn't that far from us. We arranged a bus and our hotel reservations were made. I think about eight of us went to the concert.

I was probably the oldest person in the place, in there with all those headbangers. I just loved Guns N' Roses, I thought they were a fantastic group at the time, and I wanted to go to see them. This was the first time that Guns N' Roses had played in an Eastern Bloc country, so it was quite unique, quite a nice piece of history.

The sad part was going through the border. There were so many refugees trying to get out of the country. It was quite pathetic. They were literally standing there with the clothes on their back, surrounded by their children who really didn't know what was going on, just that they were in a very unsafe place and that their mom and dad, or sometimes just one parent, were trying to get them to a safer location.

Of course, for them, the borders were closed. Hungary took in as many as they could and then said, stop, we can't keep this going. There were literally thousands and thousands a day, trying to get through the borders up there. One thing I noticed was a woman trying to give her infant child to somebody going across, obviously in an attempt to get the child to safety, even if she couldn't go. It was very sad.

The refugees we saw were mainly at the border crossings, or travelling to the border crossings. After a while they were prevented from getting to the border crossings by various means. You know genocide was a big thing over there—it was rampant while we were there but we just didn't know it. We found out when we got back how much genocide had actually been happening right under out noses, within a few kilometres of where we were.

# Afghanistan, 2003

We didn't have days off. We had a Sunday routine where you could come in at noon as opposed to first thing on a Sunday morning, so you had some time to yourself. Sunday afternoon we would break the monotony of that. We did weapons re-familiarization once a week with the different weapons that we had, to make sure people felt comfortable and didn't get complacent. Obviously the battle group didn't need to do that, they were dealing with weapons on a daily basis, but some guys didn't travel outside the camp all that often, they needed to have that familiarization so that when they did we didn't have negligent discharges or anything like that.

From a downtime point of view, some guys liked to go to the mess, some guys didn't. Even when we got the two beers per man policy in place a number of months after our Roto had gotten there, I probably had eight beers in the mess the entire six months I was there. We did PT (Physical Training) three times a week to keep us fit while we were over there—you always get fat on the staff jobs, although it's hard to get fat when you're wearing the full protective equipment with ceramic plates and weapon and helmet every time you go outside the wire, which I was doing on a daily basis.

At ten o'clock or so, we'd watch a DVD or something, or just go back to the tent and crash and do it all again. I was fortunate that my routine was broken up by the excitement of senior visitors every once in a while and meetings that I was doing, and I got out of the camp on a daily basis.

# Cambodia, 1993-94

We got some added bonuses from time to time. We helped transport some stuff in some big Russian cargo helicopters. That was nuts, just because of the level of soldier you're dealing with, the Russians at that time. I mean, they were pretty ghetto. Those Russians build aircraft to fly, they don't build them with creature comforts at all, stuff like heat. The windows were holes, so you could stick your head out the window, which was great till the sun started setting.

We got a couple of helicopter rides in Hueys and stuff like that. But most of our time was spent driving. A lot of driving.

## Afghanistan, 2006-07

Stuff like that happened, playing football, playing catch, card games that would go on all day, because people moved in and out to do their missions. Stop the card game, go fire the missions, start the card game. They would start in the morning and play till the night with their headlamps. That's all the things you do to pass the time. Anything to read was pretty valuable.

## Cyprus, 1991

When your platoon had the rest rotation, they did their stay in the Leisure Palace. It was a five-star hotel, before the war. There's a swimming pool, it's all carpeted, you have the nice big kitchen, and you have the jewellery store right there where you can get jewellery dirt cheap. So really it was a good stay. The only thing at the Leisure Palace was that you weren't allowed to drink during the week you were there. The platoon at the Leisure Palace is on call 24/7 in case there is a conflict or a riot. But you have the pool, so how can you not like it?

You rotated through every week between the section house in the buffer zone, to the platoon house, and then you'd be at the Leisure Palace. The last area we rotated to was down by a beach, so after your shift there's a 20-minute drive to the beach. Water, nice white sand, just like every picture you see of a nice Greek island.

In fact, when you had your vacation, you could go anywhere in Europe, and I decided to stay on the island for my two weeks.

Why go anywhere? I took my dive course, and I stayed at Larnaca beach because our R&R place down there was fairly cheap.

## Former Yugoslavia, 1992

To cope, we got drunk a lot, when we could. There was a bar, we were able to relieve some of the pressure, some of the stress by playing horseshoes, playing games. We had silly events, popcorn-throwing contests, that kind of thing. We'd come up with all kinds of dopey things that we would do. We would go dunking into a vat of barbecue sauce and try to retrieve various coins that were thrown in it. Things like this. Some of this was done to raise money for the family of the sergeant that was killed there.

We were able to relieve the pressure every once in a while, usually through parties. But the memory was never far from our minds. We were always vigilant of the fact that it could be someone else the next day, it could be yourself. The job we were in, we were constantly under stress.

## Cambodia, 1993-94

During Christmas, they were kind enough to send a show, with a band, and about four different singers, and a comedian, and we were literally the envy of the UN for that one. We were allowed one or two guests, and most of our guests were Australian. They brought out one girl in a skirt that—well, I've seen thongs with more material. She came out and sang "My Guy", and the guys were just drooling. Towards the end she sang, "Have Yourself a Merry Little Christmas" and I was a disaster at that point, crying like a wee girl.

Right at the end, I don't know exactly what happened, but a guy, a really quiet corporal from 2nd Service Battalion, got up on stage, and he was bombed—most of us were just smashed. So he got up on stage with his harmonica. The lights had already been turned out but the speakers were still going, and he just started playing his harmonica, and all of a sudden the whole band jumped on stage and started jamming with him. None of us knew this guy had it in him. Nobody had ever even heard him play the harmonica.

# 12

# STRESS

There is no question that any peace operation is an immense source of stress for its soldiers. The stress could come from a particular incident, or it could be the long-term exposure to danger and tension. The stress of the mission is often the defining feature of their international work—the peacekeeper's job is, by definition, never easy.

# Former Yugoslavia, 1992

Our group of four was very unique in what we did; we were out there, we were alone. The stories that we would come back to the camp with, most of the time, people didn't want to hear them. One Master Corporal became enthralled with our stories; every time we came back he would want to hear everything that had happened to us. He ended up going home after just three months. He was a total wreck because of what we had been telling him, and we got the idea we'd better keep our mouths shut; it really doesn't help us, but can do a lot of harm to other people. That sort of started the closed mouth idea. We saw what could happen if we did tell our stories, so bottling up was the norm.

There's no venting. Venting of that nature is seen as weakness—at least, that's the impression that the soldier gets. If you vent in that way you're seen as weak and unable to pull your weight, even going as far as letting down your fellow soldiers. They wouldn't trust you in a situation in the future because you had vented any kind of emotion about what you had experienced. If I were to get in the mess after one of these incidents, and break down and start crying, my credibility would be out the window.

At my rank, you were expected to set the example. I had one of my chaps come into my room one night over there. He was crying uncontrollably. I had a bottle of booze in my foot locker, and I pulled it out. This was about two o'clock in the morning. It took me about two hours to finally get the story out of him. The reason he was crying like that was because he had caused the death of a woman and her baby, or at least he felt he had.

He was up in the mountains, talking to a sniper, who was bragging to him how he could shoot somebody from over a thousand yards away. This guy basically called him on it, said no you can't, not from a thousand yards, not with that rifle. The sniper had a spotter; the spotter said there's a target there, and the sniper got down, fired, and killed a baby and the mother. The bullet went right through the baby and killed them both. They made him look at it through the high-powered telescope that they had there. He found out that day that the Serb snipers had bounties; they would get so many points if they could kill somebody like that, like a baby in its mother's arms, and if the bullet went through and killed the mother as well they got extra points. Inhumane.

# Haiti, 1995-96

Not only you couldn't sleep too well, but also you had to put 12, 16 hours a day, and deal again with all the elements, the heat, the smell, the garbage, and the dead bodies. Many occasions we used to get into a mob of people there, and I've seen people, they call it in Haiti *dechouquer*, which means to cut the person in pieces.

The law is taken in the hands of the population. If you are in a little village and you stole a chicken, well they're gonna cut your hands off. And they're gonna tie that stolen chicken around your neck. Depending how serious the offence, they would even put a tire, a used tire, around your neck full of gas and light it on fire. If your wife or husband is around, they'll do the same thing to your wife or husband. They figure if you are a thief, your wife is gonna be a thief.

On many occasions we had the chance to go there and quiet down the people and convince them that we can take the lady or the man, the thief, to prison, and have a trial done. And they'd give him into our custody, and we'll take it to the civilian police, the Haitian police and they looked after it. When you go to jail over there you have very little food. If your family doesn't bring you food then you starve to death in prison. A lot of Haitians, they'd rather die than go to prison. It was extremely hard for them too.

With depression, at the time you don't feel it because

you are so busy. First of all, we were working 16 hours a day and we were working six and seven days a week. Your system did not have the time to go into shock mode. So it was work, fight the elements, fight the smell, sleep, work. Maybe it was a good thing that we worked that hard, to help us to forget what we saw ten minutes before. But when you see a dead body flying over the hood of the truck like we had, and he's dead on the side and you're not even stopping for him, this is not normal. The human reaction isn't to react that way. You don't react that way in Canada. The first thing you do is go and see the person that got hit. In Haiti, oh well, it happens.

We got hit by another car beside us, the guy was thrown over a truck, landed, dead. We were told, things like that you just keep going. You could have been accused of hitting that person, and what do you do then? You've got a dead body there that got hit by a truck or a car, and you went and helped and then they can say, you hit him.

## Afghanistan, 2006-07

Some guys had been to Afghanistan before. You could see their nervous level go up and they became a lot more animated. For me, before I went out, I went through all those moments like, do I have the funeral arrangements that I want. I did that e-mail, the funeral e-mail, this is what I want, to my wife. You go through that. You go, wow, I could not come back, because we were so pumped up about ambushes.

But once you're out, you're in a vehicle, behind a loaded machine gun in Afghanistan, I can't say it's not a rush. You're going through the town and they say look for a white and yellow taxi, it's a suicide bomber, but there's literally hundreds of them. As you're driving through town you're looking back and forth. My buddy, I could see him in front of me, a motorcycle pulls up beside him, and he's got the machine gun pointed right at it. You never know. You're just constantly looking, looking. That vehicle has kids, that's probably okay. That vehicle has three guys, I'm not too worried. The most you can do is duck. I kept my arm in.

The right arm I always pulled in. I didn't want it ripped off. You're always thinking about those things as you're driving. But it was a rush, you're in a vehicle, it's hot, you're doing the job.

It didn't really wear us down much. We moved more than the other troops, but we weren't like the convoys that moved every day. They had suicide bomber issues. You could see they got worn down by the end. But we moved enough, we kept sharp and I think our troops were pretty good at it.

## Bosnia, 1994

It is intense, it is stressful, defusing a bomb. It's safe, you've got a sergeant telling you what to do, but the excitement is there, and in the back of the head, you know you could kill yourself. This could be the last thing you ever do if you do it wrong.

The stress level was a lot higher than when I was in Cyprus. Bosnia was like sitting on the patio watching this fight going on between the two countries and we're stuck in our camp until we're given the okay to start patrolling there, because they haven't backed off. We were waiting for them to agree to the peace and move back a kilometre on both sides so we could put the buffer zone there.

After the Medak Pocket a lot of people had issues, and that was '93 so it was '94 that they started bringing the social workers if there was an incident. After one of our losses, they actually brought us a social worker on site, and we had meeting with him as a group. That's when you start realizing that's a whole bunch of infantry guys, you're not going to get a whole bunch of those guys talking, and it's not going to happen. Because people don't want it known, I'm a tough guy. You're not going to get everyone to spill out exactly how they feel until you're alone with them.

## Afghanistan, 2003

I wouldn't say there was a general level of tension. Different people feel different things. There was a rocket strike on Camp

Warehouse that injured a contractor, and that caused an initial spike in tension, and obviously we knew that there were rockets aimed at Camp Julian. They fired those a few times but none of them actually landed in the camp. We had uncovered rockets in the King's Palace, which was just beside our camp. There was a rocket scare when the minister visited as well. There was occasionally tension but I wouldn't say there was a protracted period of stress, but then again not everyone is sort of open to talking about their stress.

## Rwanda, 1994-95

It was one day after the other, no down time. Absolutely nothing. I know sometimes the press people would bring a bottle of scotch or something in their luggage. At night they did have a little drink and sometimes they offered me some. I like beer and wine very much but I didn't have one drink at all because I wanted to keep my head in case something happened. At night when I finished those telephone calls, I would go to bed and that's it.

## Afghanistan, 2006-07

In camp, everybody has their stress level, whatever level it is. When they hit it, that's it. You could see that some of our guys were starting to approach it at certain times. We had a policy in our troop, you had to walk away. If you were being sorted by someone of a higher rank, you could walk away. And I really didn't realize it until near the end, but that's how we did it. If someone had a problem, you sort them, you let them get pissed and walk away. Because there's really nowhere for them to go.

100 metres by 200 metres. They had nowhere to go. So you had to give them that walk away and be angry time, without going after them, and let them work it out. It worked fairly well. There were times when we had to bring everybody in, if someone did something stupid, we would bring them in and sort them all out and read the riot act.

# 13

# HOME

Home never leaves the mind of soldiers abroad, and soldiers never leave the thoughts of those they have left at home. The countless family, friends, and well wishers who wait and hope for the soldiers' safe return can be as much a part of Canada's contribution to the worldwide struggle for peace as the soldiers themselves.

## Afghanistan, 2006-07

The toughest part of it was being away from my wife and baby. My daughter was born in May, so she was in her third month when I left. I mean, I've left girlfriends before to go on tour, but getting up at four in the morning in Sault St. Marie and getting on a bus to Petawawa and leaving your fiancé holding your baby of less than three months old, that was pretty hard. It was cool to come home, when I came home on leave, and just to see how big she had gotten. Huge! Missing Christmas and all that was hard too. Basically missing the family.

## Cambodia, 1993-94

The hardest thing to do was to combat monotony, combat the boredom. The girl I dated at the time was fantastic, she kept the letters coming, and so did my dad and mom. I was getting, on average, about a letter a day while I was gone, and I was cranking out at least four a week.

We went three weeks without mail at one point, and we were going off the hook. You could actually see the esprit de corps dropping. It was just before Christmas, some kind of delay in Ottawa. We actually got our bundles five days before Christmas, and a friend of mine took a picture of about 30 of his letters and packages that arrived all at once.

## Afghanistan (from Canada), 2005

We didn't talk a lot because we're not phone people. When he would phone from Afghanistan, I'd feel the need to repeat the same story five different ways. You don't want to say 'I don't want to talk to you', but you have nothing to say. You feel obligated to stay on the phone because you feel bad. For a 15-minute awkward phone call, we'd spend an hour, two hours on the computer. Funny. He'd talk and I'd be like, "Okay, can we get off the phone now so we can chat on MSN?" I just found chatting by MSN more personal.

When they're in Kandahar airport they can talk on the Internet. Out in the FOBs (Forward Operating Bases) they only have the satellite phones. He'd call on the satellite phone and we'd be talking suddenly say, "Oh, love you! Gotta go! Bye!" And he'd just hang up on me as mortar rounds are flying in. He kept lying to me and lying to me. I learned to gauge his reaction by our twins' antics. I'd tell him something they'd done and if he didn't laugh, then I'd know that he was bored. If he was happy, I was happy 'cause that means he was doing his job.

I sort of liked it when he went out to the FOB because I can live my life when he can only call me by satellite phone. We talked on the phone maybe 15 times his entire tour. But when he was in Kandahar, we couldn't get off the computer. It's amazing how much he talked on the computer.

# Cambodia, 1994

Communication home was rather difficult. We had one phone line we could use to call back to Canada; you were limited in the amount of time you could use it, and you had to pay for that time. If you wanted to call home more, you had to go downtown to one of the phone places.

They were springing up, because the Cambodians, being the ingenious people that they are—if a situation presents itself and they don't capitalize on it, it ain't worth capitalizing on. They are a country of ten million MacGyvers. They see a need and they fill it: "Oh, those guys want to call home? Well, we don't understand it, but okay, we'll put in a phone line, and by the way, that'll be six bucks US a minute, please." And people were paying it all day long.

## Afghanistan, 2003

Canada doesn't go cheap on providing services to soldiers. As a staff member I had a computer and a phone sitting at my desk all the times. I was able to pick up the phone and call home whenever I wanted to as long as it wasn't interrupting operations business. I also had minutes on the welfare phone card that I ended up never using.

It was nine and a half hours' time difference, so sometimes I actually got up at four in the morning to be able to talk with my wife. At four o'clock in the morning, you're the only one in the office tent, so you could be a little more personal in the call. I never once heard anyone complain they didn't have enough contact with back home.

If they did complain, it was more because they didn't want to call back home. There were some soldiers that didn't make regular calls and if the chain of command got advised from family centres back home, how come this husband isn't calling his wife? Are you denying him access? No, he's got a phone right there. If he chooses not to call his wife, that's not our business. You can't order guys, at three o'clock everyone will call home.

## Afghanistan, 2006-07

It was outstanding, how much talking at home you could do. We found this spot in the mountains for our satellite phone hook-ups. You only had so much time on your card in camp, and you had another card when you were outside the wire. We also used that card for the Internet. That's unprecedented. When I was in Cyprus, I had a field phone. You had to wind it to talk, and you're on this field line back to Canada. Now you can phone every night if you want. They were official phones, but basically if it wasn't being used, they opened it up.

The only time it got shut down was if someone died, and then there was a comms lockdown and no one could call home. That was so they could contact the family before everybody else could find out about it. When they had contacted the family, made sure that was all straightened out, then they'd let the comms lock end. It would last maybe a day.

I'd be talking to my wife while the artillery was firing. It was intermittent, too, and sometimes it cut out, and I'd have to reassure her, it's okay, nothing happened, I just lost the connection. At first we had the regular operational phones, then the welfare phones came out. Then the welfare computers came out. And then the guys could e-mail, they could chat, they could do everything. Facebooking near the end. They could do whatever as long as they did their work. They weren't allowed to surf porn, that was the big thing.

They encourage you to call home a lot, especially once things happened and people were dying. It was important to call and say I'm okay, I'm in a good place, to keep everybody happy. Different from my last tour, in Cyprus, where I started counting the Dear John letters, and all the relationships and marriages that broke up. On this one, hardly any, because the communication is so much better, you can talk to them so much more.

# 14

# HELP

The one recurring theme among Canadians who serve overseas is the intense compassion towards the people they encounter. The soldier's duty is always clear: help those less fortunate, and provide peace, safety, and security for all. Canada's privileged and wealthy position in the world does not create a barrier between our soldiers and the local citizens; rather, it adds to their need to assist, to give, and to console in the midst of terror, poverty, and bloodshed.

# Former Yugoslavia, 1992

One of the things I'm most proud of is that we started up a procedure where we'd go into local schools. There were so many children getting horribly mutilated from picking up and playing with explosive items that would detonate in their hands, tearing their limbs off, or they would step on things and blow their legs off and things like that. And I had kids that age myself, at that time, so it was quite heartrending.

It proved difficult starting. My translator's last name was of Serb origin. When we first went to the teachers, they all congregated in one room, about 75 teachers and the headmistress. We tried to convince them that we should come into their schools and give them the mine awareness training and advise them what the hazards were, because there was so much around them.

Their initial answer was no, you won't bring any Serb translator into our schools, we won't allow that. When the translator told me what they had said, I said, "Tell them this: I'm going to leave here and go straight over to CNN and tell them just exactly who you are and that you refuse to allow us to come in and help keep your own children safe." Of course, everybody over there watched CNN, they wanted to keep up with the news and see if their faces appeared on the news. They all looked at each other, and a couple of the drunks, a couple of the teachers that were just pissed as nits, were told to leave the room, and the rest of the teachers agreed that we could carry on and do the training with the kids.

By the time I finished there, our team, on their days off, had managed to go in and teach 4500 kids the dangers that were around there. To my knowledge, once we started doing that training, no other incidents occurred, so I was quite proud of that. And when our team left, we were replaced by a new unit, and they continued it. It stood not only for good public relations, but it also helped keep the kids over there safe. And the kids were told, take this information to your homes, your families, make sure you pass this information on to them. If you see something out there that looks anything like the items I have here on the table, don't touch it, no matter what. And try to stay off the grass.

I believe a lot of lives were saved by that effort. It was something very fulfilling for me. I guess it was mainly because I had kids myself. I took a look at these kids, what I called the innocents, being horribly maimed and injured and sometimes killed because of things that they just didn't understand, and certainly couldn't be expected to understand.

# Sri Lanka, 2005

If there's anything that affected me in any of these deployments, it's being a father, and seeing children that have nothing when you know you're trying to provide the best for your own children, when you see what children in Canada have. If anything affected me through all of my operational experience, it was the graves in Sri Lanka in the sand on the beach afterwards, and you could tell because they were shallow graves, you could smell the death there.

When you looked at the graves to pay your respects, there were graves that were very small. You got choked up inside when you know for a fact that that's not an adult grave. And it really brings it in perspective when you realize that the number of graves—over 40,000 were killed in Sri Lanka alone, they only ever found the bodies of 10,000 of them.

I can't compare it to the feeling of seeing mass graves in Bosnia because I wasn't there, but I know that affected a lot of soldiers there. But seeing thousands of graves and just knowing that there's three times that number of bodies that will never come back in, that's a very sobering thought. We kept going up and down the beach expecting to see debris and bodies coming back in from the tsunami, but nothing came back, which was sort of shocking.

Whole villages had been washed out to sea and literally there was nothing left. Concrete slabs where these houses had been, a flat piece of concrete like you expect to set your deck down on. No trace that a house, a whole community, had been there. That's a devastating thing to think of. You hear the stories and you talk to people. A fisherman, he doesn't want anything, he doesn't want money, he just wants to show you where his house used to be, where his children used to sleep.

Usually I'm quick with an answer, but that was one time I had no response. All you could say was, I'm sorry. What do you tell the guy who lost his whole family, his whole way of life? How do you show compassion when you can't really fathom what happened?

The smell of the graves, the children buried in shallow graves on the beach is something that I still remember. It's not that I can't eat chicken or anything—some people had that response to mass graves in Bosnia. But that's something I still have a strong feeling about. I can't relate to someone whose biggest issue in life is what kind of fence they're going to replace their old fence with, or I have to get a new barbeque because this barbeque just isn't cutting it for me any more. It's hard to feel sympathy for the trivial aspects of life in Canada when you've gone through those kinds of things.

## Bosnia, 1994

There were Serbs and Croatians, who were married, but the hatred between the two cultures was so bad, when the war broke out they had split up, so if you were Croatian you went to Croatia, if you were a Serb you went to the Serbian side.

On Sundays we would make a safe area between the two sides where they could come and see their family, so a father can see his kids, or the mother can see the kids, depending what side the kids went on. A lot of work had to go into that, a whole section of troops was needed to secure the area, and you never knew what was going to happen, if someone was going to take a shot at you because you're letting this happen.

## Haiti, 1995-96

When we were there we weren't thinking about dying. It was one day at a time, just like them, and we're doing well so we'll keep going. We got into a lot of trouble there, a lot of mobs and a lot of demonstrations and a lot of dirty stuff, not because we wanted to do it, but you didn't have a choice because your brain is telling you, go help.

We helped the country in the six months that I was there, I think. We discovered a lot of gangs, and turned them over to the authorities, so one less member of a gang out on the streets was one less body later on. Yes, we did a lot of good for the country. Even if later on you sit back and say the country is still the same way. And it's true and it is the same way. Today the same way as it was 10 years and 20 years ago. Will that country change? I don't know.

One thing we did was collected money and school books and school supplies and we donated it to some of the Haitian schools because they didn't have any. So that's something that we did extra for them. We helped the civilian police over there to find weapons caches and all kinds of stuff like that.

## Rwanda, 1994-95

I had never seen before what I saw in Rwanda, even in Somalia. Of course, the first few times you see scenes like that, it's terrible. Every time it's terrible. It was my job, and I went. With the press people, we would stop and the camera would film, those writing articles for the newspapers and the press agencies or whatever, they would do their job, and 20 or 30 minutes and let's get back in the truck.

One day we went to the scene of a massacre near the airport. It was not a big one, about 30 or 40 people who had been killed during the night as they were fleeing the fighting. All civilians, women, children, old men. You could see they were fleeing because most of them were on bicycles or carrying whatever they could carry. We were going to the airport that morning and we ran into this. People lying all over the road and dead in the ditches. They had just been massacred, not with machetes, with rifles or machine guns, whatever.

We stop, the journalists get out, they do whatever they have to do, and during that time what I used to do was I used to walk, I would let them do their thing. It was terrible, a woman with a little baby in her arms, both killed. I took a few photographs with my little camera. And then after that we went to the airport and then we came back to the UN headquarters. This was in the morning.

In the afternoon, maybe two o'clock, a photographer for Reuters came up to me. She was a good friend of mine, I liked her very much. She said, "I want to go back to that scene that we were at this morning." I said, "Forget it, it's too dangerous to go back, they are still fighting." She said, "I would like to go back and take some more photographs," and to make a long story short I said, "Okay, we'll go back." So she passed the word around to those press people who wanted to come, and we organized the transport, my vehicle and the little bus.

All the bodies were still there. By this time it was about three o'clock in the afternoon, it's about 35 degrees under the sun. In a couple of days, you can imagine the changes in the conditions of the bodies, but at this point they were kind of still fresh. So the press people get out of the vehicle and do whatever they have to do. I start to walk and in the ditch I see this little boy on his back, dead. He had a bullet in his thigh. Poor little guy, he was about five, six years old. I looked at him and somehow, I took my camera to take a photograph of him, don't ask me why. Believe it or not, the little guy opened his eyes and looked at me.

I almost had a heart attack. We saw this guy this morning, he'd been hit sometime the night before, and now he opens his eyes. He doesn't say a word, but he opens his eyes. Obviously he's not dead. I was with another UN officer, a guy who was driving one of the minibuses, and a guard, and I called the journalist and they came over, and of course they took photographs and started to film and this and that, and to make a long story short the little guy was alive.

We put him in the back of my 4x4 and took him back to UN headquarters. We had to go through a road block manned by rebel forces, because the rebel forces have just taken this territory. The officer in charge of the road block told me there was no way we were going to go through the road block with this little guy in my truck because this little guy was a Hutu. And I said, "No way my friend, he is coming through the roadblock and that's it." And they said, "You leave him with us, we will take care of him," and I said, "No way, you are going to leave him in the ditch and that's going to be the end of it." I mean, for them, in the middle of the war, ha!

So anyways we talked and argued and because the journalists were filming, in the end the officer in charge of the road block said I might as well let them go through instead of getting involved in a lot of problems. So we got through and I took him to the UN headquarters, and then some soldiers took him to the Red Cross hospital downtown. And with some journalists we went there a few days later, and he had already recovered, he had his femur, his thigh broken, but I'm sure now he's playing football.

# Bosnia, 2001

I got my church back home to donate a bunch of stuffed animals and send them over to me. I dubbed it Operation Bosnian Bear. They sent over four huge boxes of stuffed animals. I actually took out a patrol where I went to all the people in my patrol routes that I knew had children, and handed out stuffed animals all day long. And every one of those little kids had a smile on their face, and that alone is the reason why you're there. It's for the future generation and the fact that there's hope.

There was hope every time I was able to say yes to somebody, when they said I need this, and we happened to have it. When I can say yes, we have ten bags of beans in the back, here's a couple of bags of beans. Being able to do something for somebody, when there's so much you can't do.

I remember this Croatian woman, she was 21 years old and she had four kids. They were living on this farm that wasn't theirs, squatting really. I said, is there anything I can get you? She said, I could really use some clothes for my kids. All I have is these clothes that I found in the dumpster. Her kids were wearing clothes that she got out of the garbage. That really bothered me. So I went back to the camp, and we had some clothes that were donated but we didn't have any kids' clothes. That really upset me.

I was able to get shoes for the Serbian kids that came from Belgrade. So, yeah, the times when you can say yes, or when you can do something for somebody and they show their appreciation, that gives you your reason for being there, and I think that's the rewarding part of it.

We had, there was this one woman, she lived just on the edge of the range. And she was probably 72 years old. She had one tooth. We used to call her Grandma. Whenever you came, she'd grab your head and pull you down and give you a big kiss, the big one-two kiss. Her well was dry and she had nothing, so we went out every other day and patrolled and we took her bottles of water.

It was against policy to take a box lunch if you could avoid it because the cooks had enough to do already, but we said to the cooks, hey man, can you hook us up every other day? And they said no problem. So we'd go out and we'd share our lunch with her. She couldn't eat the apples because she only had one tooth, but whatever we could give her. Once she said, you guys are like my grandchildren. If you weren't here, I'd be dead. And that's very rewarding for someone to say to you, because of you, I'm alive.

## Sri Lanka, 2005

I got enormous satisfaction out of that mission, simply because we were there with a particular purpose in mind, a very clear mandate of what we needed to accomplish. We were more flexible than a lot of the other NGOs. People like some of the Red Cross organizations would set up camp in a particular area based on what was convenient for them, not based on what the needs of the people were. So they expected to set up a camp, and refugees would come to their location to seek medical treatment. You have to go to where the people are, particularly if you're coming a week or so after the actual event like a lot of the people were.

I was the first one to set foot in Ampara on a regular basis, and the last one to leave the camp. We pulled out late February, so I was there for just shy of two full months. Understand that the mandate of the DART, once it gets set up, is 45 days. It takes a little while to get set up. But once we start operating at the capability that we need to, 45 days later we expect to be pulled out, because we haven't got the resources in the DART to stay there longer.

We don't go there to provide immediate assistance. We don't go in there to do rescues or provide the immediate trauma medical aid to the people that have had a slab of concrete dropped on their leg or something like that. We're there to act as a bridge to carry on with that immediate aid to the point where we can turn over to rebuilding people who can then start rebuilding the bridges and the schools and things like that.

We're not there to restart the education system. We're there to clear the schools so the education system can start. It was very clear to me when I arrived that you don't go in and take over a location that needs to be used to get the people back on their feet. You don't take over a schoolyard and set up your camp there, because that then is one more school that you can't bring the schoolchildren back into.

It was sometimes difficult in Sri Lanka because the psychological effect of the tsunami caused people to be afraid of the sea that they once relied on. You have fishing villages that were wiped out, and fishermen that say they no longer want to go out to sea because they saw what the sea is capable of. They're not highly educated, so it's difficult for us to relate to that sort of thing.

It was a unique disaster. It was a long area but it wasn't

a wide area. The disaster zone affected was maybe a kilometre, two kilometres wide, and very long. Three kilometres in from the sea, it was business as usual. And a lot of the Sri Lankans there—this was something harder for our soldiers to understand—didn't want to offer aid to the people who were affected by it. They considered them squatters. They weren't paying tax on the land they were occupying by the sea. They essentially set up their own little villages to live off of the sea, but they weren't contributing to the local economy, they were looking after themselves. Some Sri Lankans didn't have much sympathy for these people and didn't want the displacement camps for these people anywhere near their buildings or towns.

That's difficult for Canadians to comprehend. I personally have been involved in flood assistance in Manitoba and was deployed to Quebec for the ice storm. We went to help any Canadian who needed our help, not to choose the ones that should have gotten help as opposed to anyone else. And that's something our soldiers couldn't understand in the psyche or the culture of Sri Lanka.

## Bosnia, 2003

When I went to Bosnia in 2003, that opened my eyes and really told me what I was doing was right. We're there for a mission and a purpose. Yeah, it takes time. In Bosnia, it didn't happen over night. It began in the 90s, but in 2003, it's established. There's still a lot of work that can be done there, not military-wise, but reconstruction. And other agencies can step into a role there.

By 2003, driving around, a lot of the houses still need to be rebuilt, but most people were not so bitter any more. Croatians and Bosnians are actually talking to each other, and actually working together to get their communities rebuilt. Things like running water to every little village, and getting electricity to all of the villages—one of the villages still didn't have electricity and they were using gas generators. I saw hydro poles actually installed by the time I left because both cultures were working together to make it happen. Back in '94 there's no way I would have told you I would have seen that.

Soldiers were taking their own time to go and help. Someone would say, let's go and help this guy finish his roof because he got some materials. Instead of sitting in camp playing floor hockey or watching a movie, we would go and spend two hours helping this guy to put his roof up. You never thought, okay, I'm done my six-hour shift and now I can rest or work out in the gym or watch TV. You'd go back out there and grab a hammer and help.

## Rwanda, 1994-95

The war ended officially on the 4th of July but it ran really until the 15th of July. Then I came back to Canada and took two weeks leave, and then I went back to Rwanda. At that time they had decided to keep me not only for two months but for a full year. At that time General Dallaire went back to Canada, and the job of spokesman was almost over, at least as a full time job, so they gave me the job of putting together a UN military police company, which would become the UN police in Rwanda.

That kept me busy almost 15 hours a day. I had to start from scratch, no people, no equipment, nothing. So I worked very hard on the education plan. Two and a half months later we had our military police company of about 75 people coming from about ten different countries with equipment, computers, everything. I was very proud of that. And I commanded that company until April 2005 and then I came back to Canada and another major from Zambia took my job. For the last six months or so that I was in Rwanda I was the commanding officer of the UN military police company which I had formed and I was very proud of that.

## Bosnia, 2001

The first few days I was on patrol, I met a family of 16 living in a half-covered house. They came out and I was talking to them. They had a little baby girl, she must have been only about one year old. She looked at me, and she smiled, and she had the biggest smile on her face.

I looked all around me, I saw the destroyed village and the squalor and the house that they were living in. And I saw the smile on her face, how her eyes lit up when she saw me. And I thought, this is the reason why I'm here. Because I can see the hatred in people's eyes, maybe not the hatred but the tiredness of it all, but I didn't see that in her eyes. I saw a normal little girl who was just excited, and who has nothing, but still has a big smile on her face. I thought, I have to keep that attitude.

Whenever I saw a burned out village or a burned out house, I tried to remember, there was a family that lived there. Something happened to that family. And it's my job to prevent this sort of thing from happening in the future.

# 15

# RETURN

For many soldiers, an unscathed return home is the happiest part of the mission. But travelling back, reuniting with loved ones, and readjusting to life in Canada present their own difficulties too, whether because home has changed while they were away, or—more often—because the veteran has changed but home has not. Certainly, mixed feelings are common when leaving a place where a soldier has worked so hard and given so much.

## Cambodia, 1993-94

You know those horror stories where the guy goes away to war and comes back and his family has moved? Yeah, that happened. I went to my mom's house and a total stranger opened the door. And I said, yeah, is Jane there, and she said oh, no, she doesn't live here any more.

She'd moved in with her boyfriend, who I'd never met. So, welcome home. The only people who knew I was coming home were my girlfriend and my dad because I wanted it to be a big surprise, and, well, surprise surprise.

## Afghanistan, 2003

When we got back home they instituted the three half-day work day. We were able to take off the day we arrived, and then the next day we were supposed to report in for work in the morning and have the afternoon off. That was for three days, and then we could take our full leave and time off.

That was designed not necessarily for soldiers to get back into a routine, but more for the families, who all of a sudden have these people arrive and be sitting there at home thinking, what am I going to do now? There were a lot of soldiers that hated it; they felt they should go on leave right away because they didn't want to g o back up to Petawawa and then travel back down to southern Ontario where family was or whatever.

I don't believe that there was a consistent problem with soldiers integrating back or being able to adapt. It was more the fact that you had to manage soldiers' spending because you can't go and drop a thousand dollars at a souvenir shop in Kabul. They got back with that kind of money in their pockets and I'm sure some of them went through their allowances pretty fast. The car dealerships in Petawawa were just loving the returning rotations.

## Haiti, 1995-96

I found it very difficult, leaving Haiti. A lot of people didn't, there are people in the military who will count their days till they come back to Canada. They're the people who are on the base all the time. Those people were living on the base and it was hot, they had to fight the heat, we had our cooks, they had their books to read at night, they had a TV, they were not in the general population of the country. So to them, the 12 hours they were working a day was extremely long. Oh, another day in the heat.

For us, it was not. One day we were here, the next day we were there, and it was moving moving moving. I get to go in town tomorrow, or I get to go here, or there, always working. You don't see the time go by. So yes, I was sad leaving the country because I was doing a lot of good.

## Bosnia, 2001

I was over there during 9/11, and they wanted to actually extend our tour because there were 15 suspected terrorists in Bosnia. Since we were already there on the ground they wanted us to stay, but I couldn't say anything. I was due to fly home on the 28th, and I was talking to my wife, and she was saying "I'm looking forward to you coming home," and I'd say "I'm looking forward to coming home," and meanwhile I can't tell her anything. Finally they decided no, they're going to do the regular rotation and you can go home on your scheduled flight. So that was a relief.

I had an incredibly different perspective, coming home. My roommate and I happened to be on the same flight back and we were up for 24 hours. We went out to the bar and we had three beers, because we could. We had no two beers limit anymore. We were dead tired and we were falling asleep on our beers, but we got our three in.

Coming back was a bit of an adjustment because I didn't want to leave. I did, but I didn't. I wanted to come home, and be normal again, and get back to my family. But I still wanted to go back to Bosnia. My wife would have none of it, and I don't blame her.

I felt like I did make a difference, and I want to keep on making a difference. I quit my civilian job three months later and started taking Class B (full-time reservist) contracts. I'm going to do that till I retire, because I'm making a difference. I'm teaching young recruits things that will keep them alive. I'm relaying experiences that I have.

## Golan Heights, 2002

The Canadian contingent was supposed to be finished soon after we left. It was really funny because it was rumours in the wind, then it was a firm deal, it's done, you guys are losing half your tour and going home. Then, cancel that, you guys are staying, but nobody's replacing you because the other countries aren't coming in. Then, that's not going to happen, they're going to send over four officers who are going to do a check of the camp and see if they can deal with it, so you'll be there another six to eight months.

It was almost a year to the time when it actually happened. And our side was saying, no, we're getting out, you'd better deal with it. It was an expensive mission, dealing with what we had to deal with, and a lot of countries just can't afford it.

## Cambodia, 1994

They were going to bring in a third tour at the end of our six months and they had a rotation all scheduled to come in, and then because of how well the mission had gone—they were calling it the most successful mission in UN Peacekeeping history—they decided, instead of bringing in a whole other rotation, we'll just keep these guys a little longer and shut the base down. So instead of keeping us for six months and bringing in another tour, which they figured would be two or three months, they just kept us there for an extra two months and never had the third tour.

Instead of having the time to get to Canada a little more slowly, we left Phnom Penh in a Herc, flew to Bangkok, changed planes and flew to Hong Kong, and then caught a Canadian Airlines flight back to Calgary. 23 ½ hours from the time we left our camp, we were stepping onto Canadian soil in Calgary.

Many guys had not left Cambodia or the Far East at all in those eight months, so it was an unbelievable shock to hit the ground inside of 24 hours, culturally and climactically. It was cold. We landed in Calgary and it was 16 degrees Celsius and we thought we'd just stepped into the Arctic, because we'd been in a jungle for eight months. We had blood thinners in us and everything else. It was quite a shocking change and they wouldn't think of doing that nowadays.

# Afghanistan, 2006-07

When I came back for leave it was kind of surreal. Driving down the highway, I didn't have to look out for suicide bombers, I wasn't behind a machine gun, and I didn't own the road. In Afghanistan you own the road, everybody gets out of the way when you're coming down the road.

We had really good decompression at the end of the tour when we went to Cyprus, although a lot of people, me included, just wanted to get home to see my family, we realized after Cyprus that it was probably a good move. People had different levels of stress. We went out drinking, did the karaoke thing. I saw a lot of other guys coming through, engineers mostly, and you could see maybe they had different levels of stress. Guys were crying in the bar, hugging each other, you saw that kind of stuff going on. Guys breaking down, and you could see their level of stress was a lot higher because they had lost people.

As we were crossing into Canadian airspace, two CF-18s pulled up beside us so we could see them, and they escorted us back. I thought that was a really good touch. They pulled up beside and a commander came on, and he said all this stuff, thanks for serving your country, and a lot of guys got choked up. I thought that was classy, that the CF-18s escorted our Airbus in.

# 16

# LOSS

In the close-knit military family, and the extended family of loved ones and friends back home, every loss is felt keenly and deeply. As a nation, we mourn every soldier who dies in foreign conflict; as soldiers, the grieving is a complex series of emotions that persists throughout every mission.

# Afghanistan (from Canada), 2005

August was the hardest month for us. We lost seven soldiers and six of those soldiers in the six days were all veterans who had been on the ground since the beginning. The seventh soldier was our neighbour. He had the same baseball statistics as my husband: three kids, 33 years old, same home base. When they were out and it happened and they came back to the FOB, all the soldiers were surprised to see my husband. They thought it was him who'd died.

It was actually the first morning that I didn't turn on the computer. I'd already been through six deaths in the last few days. I'm driving the kids to daycare and as I'm driving down the street, I notice there's a car out of place. I was thinking that must be my neighbour's parents visiting. I didn't know my neighbour or his wife except to wave on garbage day and things like that.

As I drive by, I'm expecting to see a Saskatchewan licence plate, but as I drove past, I saw that the car had a DND plate. Padres have civilian vehicles, but the plates say Canada. At that moment, I knew he was dead. And I knew that my husband was in the same place, so I didn't know if my husband was involved, and maybe dead or injured too.

I drove my kids and as I was driving home, I saw a car in my driveway out of place. It's amazing how many thoughts can run through your head in a matter of 200 metres. I was thinking, keep driving. He's not dead. If they can't find me, they can't talk to me, then he's alive, that's all there is to it. Because they only show up at your house if they're dead. They call if he's injured.

I get up to the car, and I'm already past the driveway when I realize, that's my husband's car! My mother had been there that weekend and had moved it from its usual place to the end of the driveway. The same car I've been staring at for months. The relief—I cried so hard, I couldn't even get the car into the driveway, and I was so grateful that he was spared.

I didn't know if he was injured. I didn't know what was going on. But I knew he wasn't dead because if the padres had already been to my neighbour's house before I even dropped the boys off, they would be at my house by now. I came into the house and turned on the computer and found out that it was our neighbour. Then I waited. I did not leave the house. And he finally was able to call me a day later.

# Former Yugoslavia, 1992

One of our sergeants was lost. He was a section commander, and on this particular day the troop was going out and doing reconnaissance of what we called a "black route", a dirt road. There are a lot of these in Europe. This became a patrol route for our infantry, so our engineers were assigned to go and clear the route and make sure there are no mines or booby traps along the way. They have a team that goes out in front, checking for tripwires, anti-personnel mines, anti-tank mines, anything that could be buried beneath the ground and not visible.

One of the problems was that some of the mines they were using were of a plastic nature. Very difficult to detect. And the fuses that they put into these devices have very little metal content for the mine detector to pick up. Unfortunately the mine detectors went over this location, not finding the two deeply-buried mines underneath. The sergeant was moving one of the vehicles up with the stores and replacements the unit needed, and as he moved it up, he ran over this mine location and it detonated. It hit the front right wheel, and turned the truck up and backwards, flipped it upside-down, killing him instantly.

I did the investigation on it afterwards. The crater was about a metre and a half deep. The engine was thrown 75 metres from the vehicle, and the front drive shaft was thrown about a 100 metres in the opposite direction. The vehicle itself was upside down and facing backwards, against a tree.

We took the vehicle back to the camp and did forensic scrapings in the area where we thought the explosive content might give us some evidence, and sure enough, it came out that it was one of these mines that is very, very difficult to detect because there is almost no metal content. So no blame on the people who searched the area, no blame on the equipment. It was a very unfortunate incident.

It was significant because it proved to us that the mine detectors that we had weren't sufficient, they weren't good enough to find all the things that were in the ground. We had to go back to the drawing board and find something that actually worked. So Defence Research got working on it and everybody started being more vigilant of course. But you could not fault the engineers that did the initial search.

Very, very sad. I knew the chap, I was very good friends with him. He was a long-distance marathon runner, and he also was the same specialty as me, in explosive ordnance disposal. Him and I had gone on courses together and on trials, and in his family he had two lovely young girls. His wife attended the November 11th parade that year.

## Afghanistan, 2006-07

Our battery was actually very lucky. One guy fell down some stairs and broke a leg, but otherwise our battery literally lost no one. Every other company, everyone was losing. 19 died on our tour. One was the RSM (Regimental Sergeant-Major). Everybody knew him. He was a figurehead, number one soldier, super soldier, RCR (Royal Canadian Regiment), Airborne guy. He had really pumped up the troops and was very charismatic.

And he was just gone because the insurgents changed tactics. Instead of blowing up right next to our vehicles, they realized that wasn't working, so they blew up eight metres away so the shrapnel would hit the guys on top instead. I think that's how they got him.

It definitely had an affect on us because he was always in front of us. One CSM (Company Sergeant-Major) had to go home.

He was real close to the RSM and he just couldn't go on after that. It was weird because I knew him, he was a typical hardcore infantry guy, but it was just too much for him. He went home on leave and he just didn't come back. Everybody has their limit.

# Afghanistan, 2003

We obviously had our casualties there. There were three of them. I won't say there were only three, every casualty matters to you. At that time Canadians back home were indifferent to it, or more supportive of what we were doing, so we didn't have the feeling that people would be saying back in Canada, pull the troops out, every time one of our soldiers died.

In most missions, you get there, you're initially uncomfortable, then you start to build up a comfort factor. Then in October we had the mine strike that killed two soldiers. Now that wasn't an accident; you might as well call it an attack on our soldiers. And that's the way we very much viewed it because those mines were planted there in order for that vehicle to hit it. Feelings could go up a notch that way. And then our rotation rolled into Christmas, and then morale is down a little bit because you're spending Christmas away from your family. So a bit of a low tide at Christmas, and then a high tide at New Year's when the Governor General came.

Then a couple weeks later Corporal Murphy's suicide bombing death. And then the day we're having the memorial service for Corporal Murphy in theatre, we hear the explosion across the other side of town, which killed a British soldier. So then you start thinking, is this the way the mission is going in Kabul. Because apart from the attack in October, we hadn't seen a lot of direct action against us, then it looked like it started to go up.

I was leaving in February and Corporal Murphy died in January, so I wasn't there long enough after he died. That was one of the significant times when support for our mission started to go because he was really the first casualty to be caused by a suicide bomber, and it shook us because it happened in the same spot where we drove back and forth every day.

I never personally met any of the three soldiers we lost on my rotation, but when you attend the memorial ceremony for them, you're their brother. Every soldier is your brother over there, and I felt in a lot of ways closer to the soldiers there even if I didn't know them, because we'd gone through the same sort of training I had, the same sort of outlook, the same sort of focus on what we'd been doing for the past six months, more than I had with any of my real brothers back home. So it sounds corny, but the whole concept of a band of brothers is very much true in the military. And it's particularly true on operations, especially when you have soldiers that don't come home.

# 17

# AFTERMATH

The many traumas that soldiers experience are difficult to deal with at the time they occur, and their effects can last a lifetime. Both physical and emotional scars—physical disabilities, depression, family difficulties, and post-traumatic stress disorder—are common in soldiers who return from "hot" zones. The symptoms range from small adjustments in attitude and outlook to long-term mental and physical affliction; each soldier bears the burden of experience in his or her own way.

# Rwanda, 1994-95

I never really had time to think of what was happening, to tell you the truth. Those people that say they were affected so much by this or by that, and of course General Dallaire himself and some other people. I've said maybe I was crazy already, it was possible.

I arrived in Rwanda in April 1994 and I came home in April 1995, and I took some leave and then I left the forces. I found it very depressing all of a sudden. You leave Rwanda, you end up in your house, and the only thing you have is to cut the grass. Then I had some very black ideas and so on, but I was very fortunate because I applied with the UN as a civilian and I was hired immediately and given a very good job. I went back to Africa immediately, in some other countries, and I stayed with the UN until 2004. That helped me to make the transition between the military and the civilian life.

If I had stayed in my house or had some little military job, in some office from eight to four, having all the time to think about all these bad things, I don't know what would have happened to me. I was immediately sent back to Africa, I travelled from one country to another, a big job with a lot of responsibilities, and maybe it helped me.

Of course some things come back to haunt me about Rwanda and I'll give you just one example. I cannot go into a supermarket and look at the meat counter. Of course I can look at it, I bought some hamburgers a few times, but I don't want to look at raw meat. It reminds me too much of the raw meat that I saw in Rwanda, the raw meat of human beings. This is just one example.

It affects me, I'm sure, but maybe not as much as some

other people. Thank God that I was in good health and I managed to sleep regardless of what I had seen. When you see a little boy who was just beaten with a hammer and left for dead and he is still alive—I could tell you stories like that for the rest of the day. You've seen the worst that humanity can do to another human being. Animals don't even do that to each other.

# Haiti, 1995-96

When I came back to Canada, going back to my normal job, I found myself useless, I was no good for nothing any more. I went through a depression because I didn't know what to do with myself. Everything I was doing, my normal routine work, it was nothing to me. It was just boring. Before I went to the mission, my job in Canada was hard but I had to do it. But when I came back to Canada I felt useless. I felt that when we were in Haiti we were doing a lot of good for the country. I actually asked to go back to Haiti for another six months. But the policy in Canada is you have to be in country for a year before you are deployed again.

I didn't get treatment when I came back to Canada. We're talking 1996 here. When I came back to Canada I did my medical, I was fit, I went back to work. If we felt that something is wrong with us, we could go and see a counsellor, but myself, I never went.

I don't wake up in the middle of the night with flashbacks. But I do think about Haiti and I do think about what I did almost every day. What we did over there in that country is not what a normal Canadian does. Not even a police officer that is on the streets every day. Totally different. It was nothing to drive down the street and hear shots and the car beside you being shot at. How often are you going to run into this? Yes, you might see this in Toronto once, twice a year, and it's one person. You're not talking gangs and you're not fighting the heat and the garbage. It's a totally different atmosphere.

I think about Haiti all the time. Will that catch up with me later on in my life? Possibly. Not in the near future because I'm too busy with my business, I don't have time to sit down and think. However, when my business was quiet for three months, I tended to go down into depression again. I'm useless, I'm not doing anything. Many times I have tried to apply for UN work again, because once you live that you know you're doing good. You want to go and help people.

At the present time I don't think I have time for depression and things like that. But later on, you never know.

# Cambodia, 1993-94

I had no idea what I was going to do when I got home, not a clue. I thought I was just going to take the world by the balls, go to college, but I was so used to the military pace of things, with the automatic gratification. You know, you work your balls off for a day, and you get to see the end result. Then I'm going to school where there's studying involved, so I didn't do well there. I was just in a state of limbo for the next year, just no idea what direction I was going in. Back then, there wasn't a lot of re-engagement into society. Somalia opened that all up, and Somalia got back just after us. Back then, you just came home.

I came home a lot more disciplined, I came home with a much better work ethic. I just had no time for laziness at all. The next thing they sent me on, the next year, was my Combat Leader's Course, and if I found any kind of laziness or weakness, I would just tear it apart. It was just so stupid. Old school stupid, I guess.

There was a certain rush, I guess. Every day you had purpose, you were there for a reason. We knew why the mission was going on, and it was a mission that every soldier completely believed in. There was no question about what we were there for. But because it was a transport battalion, it was like a job. You did your ten, twelve hours a day and that was it, you were done. There wasn't the crazy go-go-go-go all the time. But at least you had a sense of purpose. And when you come home and you no longer have that purpose, that became a letdown.

I might sound like a big wimp, but the easiest way to get rid of the depression or the anger or the boredom was to just have a beer at the end of the day. And the one turned into ten which turned into 20, and next thing you know I was drinking five nights a week. When I came home, I was still in that mindset.

So when I got home and I met up with my girlfriend, here I've been away for six months and now I've got to get inundated with all this information about what I've missed. And then the problems that people had, that they complained about, just the civilian mindset that I was back in with, was just so trivial. Coming back from seeing what I'd seen and having done what I'd done, my response was, what are you complaining about. And I would get angry and stupid about it really quick.

I can remember at the home regiment, they had a big welcome home party for the bunch of us who came home together. We were drinking away, and I made some chauvinist comment. I don't even know who the girl was, she looked at me and played pokey-chest with me, with the "you just think you're so cool because you got a UN tour." I just lit up. I screamed and yelled and ranted and raved like a moron until she was crying. Once she was crying, of course, I started to really poke so I could disintegrate her.

When I left she was being consoled out in the stairwell, there, and she yelled out to me, "Are you leaving?" and I said, "Yeah," and she said, "I hope you get hit by a car out there," and I said, "Well I know it'll be a woman driver." That was what a moron I was at the time. I don't suffer from PTSD by any stretch of the imagination. I just had to find my loop again.

## Qatar, 1990

There really wasn't any debriefing for any kind of stress. Then people started coming down with what they called "Stress Syndrome", or "Gulf War Syndrome". Symptoms started to show up—myself, I didn't have any; I was asked, but in those days they weren't that well set up to bring people down from the stress that they'd been under, and re-integrate them back into their families and so on.

You can imagine, over the months, your wife has gotten

quite used to running the house by herself. You've come out of an area that's exceptionally hot, you've been drinking enormous amounts of water every day, living in very poor conditions. Now you're brought back, there's no stress, so the tendency is to hit the bar and hit it hard. A lot of drinking and thank god I'm alive type feeling, *joie de vivre*, I call it.

You'd get into a bottle for a little while, then you'd want to go to the mess and be with your buddies, and your wife couldn't understand this because one of the problems in coming out of an area like that is you can talk to people who've been there and gone through it with you, but you go back to your home and try to tell people who hadn't been there these stories and they just look at you like you're nuts. They don't believe you or they can't comprehend what you're trying to tell them. There's a significance for you that's hard to transfer to somebody else.

## Bosnia, 2001

I was really bitter to the general Canadian population for a long time. I held it against them that they didn't care, that they could watch something on TV and turn it off. For 30 seconds they say oh, that's really sad. And then go about their daily business. Or when I'm standing in line at the supermarket and the guy behind me is getting pissed off because the lady in front of me had never used a debit card before, and he has some place to be.

Even with people at my church. I was quite a regular member and very committed, and while I was in Bosnia I read the Bible cover to cover. I got home and started going back to church, and I didn't want to be around these people. They're praising God, and saying how great life is and everything, and I've been to a godforsaken place. I held it against them.

I was really reclusive. All I wanted to do was to go out and drink with my buddies. Everyone asks you questions. How was your tour? I just got back from six months of all this, and you want me to talk about it. I just wanted to drink with my buddies because they know better, that if I want to talk, I'll talk. If I don't want to talk, I won't talk. And they don't ask questions.

I came back and thought everything was different, but it wasn't. Everything else was the same, I was different. People were just going about their daily lives. It took me a long time to realize that I can't hold that against them because they don't know any better.

If something's going on in the Middle East and I see it on the TV, I can change the channel and not be affected. But if I hear something on Bosnia and if something's going down, I can't sleep for days, because I lived it. I know the people, I know their plight. I'm no different from anybody else because I can turn other stuff off. I just can't turn that off.

## Cambodia, 1994

I know that it affected a number of people. It affected me to an incredible degree. Not to the point where I shut down and became no longer a functioning member of society, but I'm not the same person I was when I went over there. It's only been the last four or five years where I could sit down and quantify how it changed me. I knew I wasn't the same person, but I couldn't tell you how or why. I'm sure there's a number of people that are like that.

I've got a friend who's been diagnosed with PTSD from a number of other missions. And I remember we were sitting down and talking about it one day and he brought one of these questionnaires from a psychiatrist. I think there were about 30 or 40 questions on it. If you answered so many questions this way, they'd put you in this category, you know, high risk for PTSD. I went through the questionnaire and I was right at the top of the heap for PTSD. I've never looked at it as that. Certainly, I never sought any medical attention for it. But definitely the tour changed me entirely. It changed the very person that I am. Some ways good, but some ways not so good.

## Former Yugoslavia, 1992

Not being able to tell those stories and relate those feelings means they end up staying with you. Nowadays they have very good procedures for sending people over; it takes several days to approve a chap going over, nowadays but back then they just pointed at you and said, you're going. When you came back, they said, welcome back, you can have two weeks off and then back to your desk.

After my tour in Yugoslavia, after six months of being in war-like conditions, being fired at, shelled, and bombed, and seeing all the things that we did see over there, the reintegration was quite poor. The Canadian Forces didn't have the capability to reintegrate us properly and efficiently. Nowadays, you find that a lot of people have had post-traumatic stress disorder.

We had a short visit with a team of medical people. We had about a 20-minute visit with them, and they said something to the effect that, when you go home, remember your wife hasn't been with you for six months, and it's going to be quite difficult, so take it easy on her the first time you have sex. That was all the briefing we got from them. I'm glad to see that things are going much better nowadays.

The group that I was with was a unique group, no one really knew how much danger we were in. In the areas we were driving through there were always snipers on the roads. You could imagine driving through the mountains, you just get this feeling in the centre of your forehead that somebody is pointing a rifle at you. You have this feeling the whole time you're there.

I was a very heavy drinker for a long time, in those days and after I got out of the military. I drank and drank and it was literally to enjoy life. I was so glad I got out of there and got out alive, with all my fingers and toes. I was just partying, partying, partying, and things were going downhill very quickly for me.

About three or four years after I got out of the military I realized that I was killing myself, and I quit drinking cold turkey, just stopped. I haven't had a drink since. When I came out of the bottle, you might say reality took over and I started realising the enormity of what I had gone through. I started having dreams and nightmares and things like that.

Post-traumatic stress disorder was not something you talked about in the military, it was something that you just put up with. That carried on into my civilian life as well. Wherever I went,

I just didn't talk about it. But even if I could, who would I talk to? Who could I relate to who would understand it? Nobody could comprehend it. Even my own family, there was no way I would burden my wife or my son with the information I had.

I started looking around, I started asking questions about whether there was a group of ex-military people I could get involved with, and there wasn't. One day I got an e-mail about post-traumatic stress disorder, and I said, I've got that! That's me! I realized that these feelings that I had actually had a name. So I called Veterans Affairs. They said they could send me to a counsellor if I wanted, and I said sure, send me to a counsellor.

So they sent me to this young woman in the local area, and unfortunately she wasn't qualified to deal with what I was telling her. She admitted it; she was just blown away. I was supposed to have five sessions with her, that's what Veterans Affairs paid for. She gave me seven. But by the time seven rolled around, I told her look, this isn't helping me in the least. I need to get in with a group that has similar experiences, that will understand and be able to relate to and comprehend what I'm telling them.

Then I heard about a group that was getting together, sponsored by the Legion. I actually got to sit and talk to people who had had similar experiences. In fact, one of the chaps had been in the Medak Pocket, so he knew exactly what had been going on in Sarajevo and the surrounding area. The doctors and the psychiatrist in the group had being doing this for ten years, so they had a lot of experience in listening to our stories and helping us work through it.

One of the things that I worked through with them was that story where I had to man the .50 cal machine gun and the possibility that I would have to kill that woman. It loomed pretty large. I didn't realize it, but that seriously bothered me for many years. I'd been harbouring these feelings and these fears for all that time.

They re-enacted it, and during the re-enactment I broke down in tears. I became extremely emotional and it just all vented. It was very, very helpful. That was one of maybe a dozen that I should go through. Unfortunately, they can only do so much at these group sessions.

My biggest problem is dreams, my lack of sleep at night. When I go to bed, I'll sleep for about two to three hours quite well, and then suddenly wake up. For the rest of the night I'm seeing visions, or I'm replaying events sort of in a sleepy haze. That's why I'm now retired. I live about 70 miles from where I worked, and in my job I took a company car and drove all over. I had fallen asleep many times while I was driving, so I decided before I killed someone I'd better quit, and I retired early. I'm in my early sixties and I'm totally retired from work.

I've not applied for anything, although at my last group session I was told that I should, and I might consider it because I could have continued working until I was 70 if I'd wanted to, and I was pulling in a pretty good wage. Now I'm reduced to just my army pension and CPP. It is a financial difficulty. I was told that if I went and asked for some assistance, I could get it. It seems easy, but then it's still a source of pride for me.

Each time you have an incident afterwards, your mind gets damaged more. It's cumulative, and eventually, it comes back at you. These chaps that are in Afghanistan now, you're going to find an awful lot of them coming out with stress disorder, and they're going to need to be looked after for a long time. They're going to be going back into a civilian life, and lost. That's what happened to me, I hope that doesn't happen in the future.

# Appendix: Canadian Missions

The following are brief descriptions of the international missions in which Canada has participated from the end of the Cold War to the present day.

### 1965-98, Cyprus

Canada's longest UN Peacekeeping mission to date was created to prevent recurrence of fighting between the Greek Cypriots and Turkish Cypriots in the ongoing dispute over the island of Cyprus. Canada guarded the buffer zone separating the belligerents for over three decades, including during the Turkish invasion of Cyprus in 1974.

### 1974-2002, Golan Heights

A Canadian contingent was sent to the buffer zone of the Golan Heights between Israel and Syria, providing communication, logistics and technical support for the UN force. 226 Canadian personnel were deployed at its inception, and over 12,000 personnel served in the Golan Heights throughout the mission.

### 1990-91, Qatar

After Iraq's invasion of Kuwait, Canada participated in a coalition of countries to force Iraq out, establishing bases in Doha, Qatar to operate and support a squadron of CF-18 aircraft.

### 1992-93, Cambodia

This mission monitored the ceasefire in place between government forces and the Khmer Rouge, and to assist with and oversee the first democratic elections held in Cambodia for decades. Later, the mission to Cambodia included the mandate to establish mine awareness, as well as to monitor disarmament and cantonment of factions. Approximately 240 Canadian Forces personnel served at any given time.

## 1992-94, Somalia

Canada entered Somalia with 20 other nations to provide assistance in relief, economic rehabilitation, judiciary systems and political reconciliation to a country that had been ravaged by over 20 years of civil war and lawlessness. During the mission, Canada contributed up to 900 Canadian Forces members at any given time, including Headquarters staff and officers.

## 1992-present, Former Yugoslavia

Canada was a major contributor of personnel, equipment, and expertise throughout the numerous UN and NATO missions in the former Yugoslavia, from the first forces deployed to the region in February 1992 to the present day. Canadian personnel have been present throughout the region, including operations in Croatia, Bosnia, Kosovo, and Serbia and Montenegro, maintaining security and delivering humanitarian aid.

## 1994-97, Rwanda

This mission was established to provide security and protection of displaced persons, refugees and civilians at risk in Rwanda as well as to provide support for the distribution of relief supplies and humanitarian relief. Canadian Lt.-Gen. Roméo Dallaire led this mission to supervise the warring Tutsi and Hutu population. Canada provided a logistics support unit of up to 112 Canadian Forces personnel.

## 1995-96, Haiti

This mission was established to create a secure environment and train a Haitian National police force, as well as to provide electoral support. Canada provided up to 500 military personnel and approximately 100 civilian police throughout the mission period.

### 1998-99, Central African Republic

Canada's maintained security and stability in the capital city, helped deliver a short-term police training program, and assisted and supported national elections. Over 50 Canadian personnel were present during the national elections of 1999.

### 2002-present, Afghanistan

Following September 11, 2001, Canada has been the largest participator in the NATO-led invasion of Afghanistan, after the United States and the United Kingdom. Approximately 15,000 Canadian troops have been stationed in Afghanistan since 2002, with over 2000 Canadian personnel in Afghanistan at any given time.

### 2004-05, Sri Lanka

Canada's Disaster Assistance Response Team (DART), consisting of approximately 200 Canadian Forces staff including doctors, engineers, and technicians, provided disaster relief following the Indian Ocean tsunami from the end of December 2004, until February 2005.

# ACKNOWLEDGEMENTS

Thank you, first and foremost, the Canadian veterans who gave their time so generously, and who talked so candidly about their experiences. Each and every contribution is appreciated and I am privileged to have talked to so many of you. I hope this book demonstrates my immense respect and honour for your commitment and sacrifice.

I am deeply indebted to the Canadian Association of Veterans in UN Peacekeeping, the Memory Project, and the Canadian Peacekeeping Veterans Association for their help in putting me in touch with veterans across Canada. Ron Griffis and Jill Paterson were especially helpful in finding veterans to interview, and I could not have completed this project without their generous help.

My publisher, Robert Morgan, and BookLand Press have been exceptional from the initial discussions about the project, through the difficulties in pulling it together, to this finished book. The support, encouragement, and enthusiasm have been tremendous. To me, BookLand Press represents the best of publishing in Canada, and I am thrilled and honoured to be part of the BookLand Press family.

Jacqueline Kreller was of invaluable assistance to me in a very difficult part of this project, and I am grateful for her speedy, diligent work.

I deeply appreciate all the interest that members of the media have given this project, including Ian Darling and Kevin Swayze of the Kitchener-Waterloo Record, and Nicole Lampa of CTV News.

I have received support from many, many members of the Canadian Authors Association and the Dove Tale Writers. I am especially thankful for the encouragement of my fellow writers Marianne Paul, Sandra Stewart, Nancy Morrey, and Suzanne Harris, as I have depended on them to keep me positive throughout this project.

The support of my close friends and family in this project has been nothing short of tremendous. I continue to draw strength and perseverance from their excellent examples.

Finally, as always, my wife SuMei has been incomparable in her unflagging support and encouragement. She puts up with the worst of this, makes it all better, and these few words cannot adequately convey my love and gratitude.

## ABOUT THE AUTHOR

Matthew Bin is a writer living in Cambridge, Ontario. He served as a Bombardier in the 11th Field Regiment, Royal Canadian Artillery, from 1991 to 1994. He graduated from McMaster University, earning a BA in English in 1996 and an MA in English in 1997.

Matthew is currently the president of the Waterloo-Wellington branch of the Canadian Authors Association. His first novel, *LMF*, was published by Little Green Tree Press in 2006. His articles have appeared in various national and international magazines, including *American Atheist, Inside Soccer Canada*, and *InBurlington*.

# ALSO AVAILABLE FROM BOOKLAND PRESS

- *Twice in a Blue Moon*
  by Marianne Paul
  ISBN: 978-0-9783793-3-9

- *Karen Cockburn: Soaring High*
  by Martin Avery with Karen Cockburn
  ISBN: 978-0-9780838-8-5

- *Where Lives Take Root*
  by Christina Kilbourne
  ISBN: 978-0-9780838-9-2

- *Tending Memory*
  by Marianne Paul
  ISBN: 978-0-9780838-5-4

- *Alexandra Orlando: In Pursuit of Victory*
  by Martin Avery with Alexandra Orlando
  ISBN: 978-0-9780838-2-3

- *The Roads of Go Home Lake*
  by Christina Kilbourne
  ISBN: 978-0-9780838-1-6

For ordering information, please visit
www.booklandpress.com
or call 1-800-535-1774